Briefly: Descartes' *Meditations on First Philosophy*

Briefly: Descartes' *Meditations on First Philosophy*

David Mills Daniel

scm press

The author and publisher acknowledge material reproduced from
René Descartes, *Discourse on Method and Meditations on First Philosophy*,
translated by Donald A. Cress, fourth edition, Indianapolis/Cambridge:
Hackett Publishing Company, 1997, ISBN 0872204200. Reprinted by
permission of Hackett Publishing Company, Inc. All rights reserved.

British Library Cataloguing in Publication data

A catalogue record for this book is available
from the British Library

0 334 04091 4/978 0 334 04091 0

First published in 2006 by SCM Press
9–17 St Alban's Place,
London NI ONX

www.scm-canterburypress.co.uk

SCM Press is a division of
SCM-Canterbury Press Ltd

Printed and bound in Great Britain by
Bookmarque Ltd, Croydon, Surrey

Contents

Contents

Introduction

The SCM *Briefly* series is designed to enable students and general readers to acquire knowledge and understanding of key texts in philosophy, philosophy of religion, theology and ethics. While the series will be especially helpful to those following university and A-level courses in philosophy, ethics and religious studies, it will in fact be of interest to anyone looking for a short guide to the ideas of a particular philosopher or theologian.

Each book in the series takes a piece of work by one philosopher and provides a summary of the original text, which adheres closely to it, and contains direct quotations from it, thus enabling the reader to follow each development in the philosopher's argument(s). Throughout the summary, there are page references to the original philosophical writing, so that the reader has ready access to the primary text. In the Introduction to each book, you will find details of the edition of the philosophical work referred to.

In *Briefly: Descartes' Meditations on First Philosophy*, we refer to René Descartes, *Discourse on Method and Meditations on First Philosophy*, translated by Donald A. Cress, fourth edition, Indianapolis/Cambridge: Hackett Publishing Company, 1998, ISBN 0872204200.

Each *Briefly* begins with an Introduction, followed by a chapter on the Context in which the work was written. Who was this writer? Why was this book written? With some Issues to Consider, and Some Suggestions for Further Reading, this *Briefly* aims to get anyone started in their philosophical investigation. The detailed summary of the philosophical work is followed by a concise chapter-by-chapter Overview and an extensive Glossary of terms.

Bold type is used in the Detailed Summary and Overview sections to indicate the first occurrence of words and phrases that appear in the Glossary. The Glossary also contains terms used elsewhere in this *Briefly* guide and other terms that readers may encounter in their study of Descartes' *Meditations on First Philosophy*.

Context

Who was René Descartes?

The rationalist philosopher, René Descartes, sometimes called the 'founder' or 'father' of modern philosophy, was born in La Haye (now 'Descartes') in Touraine, in 1596. After attending the Jesuit Collège of Henri IV at La Flèche, he studied law at the University of Poitiers, although he never practised as a lawyer. In 1618, he became a soldier in the army of Prince Maurice of Nassau, who was fighting to free the Netherlands from Spain. Descartes' aim in doing so was to travel and widen his experience, rather than to follow a military career; and his time as a soldier gave him the opportunity to think about philosophy and mathematics. The latter appealed to Descartes (who was a distinguished mathematician), as it offered certainty; and he hoped to find something certain in philosophy as well. In 1628, he settled in Holland, where he lived for the next 20 years, and concentrated on philosophical and scientific study. In 1634, he decided to suppress his treatise on science, *The World*, because he feared that the Roman Catholic Church would condemn its Copernican ideas, just as it had Galileo's. He published his *Discourse on the Method to Rightly Conduct the Reason and Search for the Truth in Mathematics* (the *Discourse on Method*), which dealt with a range of scientific issues, as well as indicating how he would carry out

his philosophical programme (it contains his famous statement, *Cogito ergo sum*: 'I think, therefore I am') in 1637; and
the *Meditations* in 1641. These were followed by *The Principles
of Philosophy* (1644), setting out his main philosophical ideas,
and *The Passions of the Soul* (1649), dealing with the issue of
how soul and body interact. In 1649, Queen Kristina invited
Descartes to Sweden, to teach her philosophy, but he devel-
oped pneumonia there and died in 1650.

What are the *Meditations on First Philosophy*?

In his *Meditations*, Descartes searches for something absolutely certain, which will provide a secure base for all knowledge. However, in his Letter of Dedication to the Dean and
Doctors of the Faculty of Theology at the Sorbonne, in which
he seeks their endorsement of his book, Descartes makes it
clear where he wants his philosophical investigations to lead.
God's existence and the immortality of the soul must be
proved philosophically. It is no good referring non-believers to
God's revelation in the Bible, and asking them to accept it on
faith, because only philosophical proofs will convince them.
By proving God's existence and the immortality of the soul,
he believes he will serve 'the cause of God and religion'. In
fact, as he explains in the Synopsis, the book does not contain
a detailed proof of the soul's immortality, but of an essential
prerequisite of doing so – that the soul is completely distinct
from the body, is pure substance and indivisible, and so is
unaffected by bodily death. After writing the *Meditations*, Descartes invited objections from philosophers and theologians,
including Thomas Hobbes, and the book was published with
these objections and Descartes' replies (this *Briefly* covers the
Meditations only, but the objections and replies are available:

see Suggestions for Further Reading). The book was written in Latin and, in the preface, Descartes explains the dangers of writing about complex philosophical issues in a language (like French) that the majority can read – it may encourage ignorant people to believe (falsely) they can understand them.

But where should Descartes begin? As he is looking for certainty, it is no good building on shaky foundations. He acknowledges (**Meditation One**) that many of his beliefs are based on sense experience, but his senses sometimes deceive him. It seems impossible to doubt, for example, that he is now looking at his own hand. But, when asleep, he dreams he is doing all sorts of things that he is (or thinks he is) not; and there is no infallible way of distinguishing what he sees in dreams from what he sees when awake.

But is this a reasonable point? People do not find it hard to tell the difference between dreams and reality. As Descartes points out, later in the *Meditations*, events in dreams do not follow a predictable pattern. However, there is room for doubt, which puts a question mark over all sense experiences. But what about mathematical truths? Two plus three always make five. However, an all-powerful God may have so arranged matters that, although the earth and its contents do not exist, they appear to. There is no reassurance in the view that God is supremely good, because this suggests he would not allow people to be mistaken at all, which is not the case.

The commonsense response is to ask what difference so comprehensive a delusion would make. If everything looks the same, and the world seems to go on functioning, why worry? However, for Descartes, the possibility of his being deceived is not compatible with the certainty he is seeking. Until he has removed this possibility, he must withhold assent from all his former beliefs, however probable. He will conduct himself as if an evil demon is deceiving him, treating external objects as illusions, and regarding himself as without body or senses.

Thus, we have Cartesian doubt, a comprehensive doubt that embraces everything that can possibly be doubted, including the existence of the external world. It was not a new idea. Publication of the writings of the second-century Greek philosopher, Sextus Empiricus, in the sixteenth century, had popularized the ideas of the Greek sceptic, Pyrrho of Elis. Thus, Descartes did not invent total, or Pyrrhonic doubt, as an approach to philosophical enquiry. But why should such a doubt arise? It seems an extraordinary attitude to adopt, but does pick up a feature of human experience – that we have no direct knowledge of other people's minds or thoughts, so it is possible (although pointless) to maintain that only ours exist. Is it sustainable? It seems unlikely. Somebody who claimed to hold such a view would belie it every time he behaved as if people and objects in the external world actually exist.

Having put himself in this position, how can Descartes move forward? Although our senses sometimes deceive us, we use the information we receive from them to correct our mistakes. However, total doubt makes progress impossible. One approach is to accept that it is possible to doubt everything, but to recognize that this need have no practical effect on the way we lead our lives and the use we make of sense experience.

But this will not do for Descartes, who wants absolute certainty. And now (**Meditation Two**) he identifies a point of certainty – that he is thinking. Even if an all-powerful God is deceiving him, he exists, if he is being deceived. He is not nothing as long as he is conscious of himself as something that thinks (the 'I think, therefore I am' of the *Discourse*). Thinking cannot be separated from him, so he can be certain that he is a thinking thing. Thus, for Descartes, knowledge starts with consciousness/thought and the mind (rationalism), not sense experience (empiricism). He uses a piece of wax to illustrate the point that (despite his instincts to the contrary), he understands himself better than external objects. At first, hard and cold, wax becomes soft and pliable when heated. However, his realization that wax can change does not come through his senses, but through mental inspection and judgement, so there is nothing he perceives with less difficulty than his own mind.

He now (**Meditation Three**) clearly and distinctly perceives that he is a thinking thing, and feels that he can take it as a general rule that what he clearly and distinctly perceives is true, but where does he go next? He has ideas of things that seem to come from external objects, and is naturally inclined to think they do, but as he has chosen to doubt the existence of the external world, there is no way he can discover, from the experiences themselves, whether or not they have an external source. He is locked inside his own thoughts, with no way of breaking out.

However, he has no evidence that God deceives. It was his idea to suppose he did; and the idea that he has of an infinite and omnipotent creator God seems more real to him than those of finite things. An effect (in this case, his idea of God) cannot come from nothing; nor can its cause be less perfect than the idea itself. As this is of an infinite God, it cannot have originated in his own mind, as he is finite. Therefore, it must have come from an infinite being. Further, as a finite being, he is aware of the defects of his own finitude by contrasting them with his idea of an infinite being and its perfections, while this idea is the most clear and distinct he has. So, God must exist.

5

Descartes does not leave it at that. He explores the possibility that his idea of the perfections of an infinite being may originate in his own mind, because he possesses them potentially. But perfection is not achieved incrementally; there is nothing potential in God, so his idea of a being more perfect than himself must come from one who is. Also, as a thinking thing, if he had got his being from himself, and/or had the power to ensure his continued existence, he would be aware of it. He could not exist, and have the idea of God, unless God existed. As he is aware of his own defects, he recognizes his dependence on a thinking thing that possesses all perfections, and who is his sole cause (among God's perfections are his unity and simplicity) and preserver. Such a being does not deceive, because deception is a defect.

Having established God's existence, Descartes can now move on to knowledge of other things. As God is not only no deceiver, but an infinitely powerful creator God, who possesses all perfections, this should solve the problem of how to move from ideas that seem to come from external objects to the existence of an external world – God can guarantee that it exists. But how convincing is Descartes' 'principal argument' for God's existence? Why should we accept his claim that the idea of a supremely perfect being can only come from a being who is? It may be another reason to think there is a God, but it is not compelling proof that he exists. Instead of agreeing with Descartes that we are aware of our own imperfections by contrasting them with our (God-given) idea of an infinite being and its perfections, we may think that we develop the idea of an infinite being from imagining ourselves as immortal and free of the limitations of physical existence.

But, why (**Meditation Four**) did God not make human beings incapable of making mistakes? One (convenient) answer

Descartes gives is that an infinite God does things that finite human minds can never understand. It is easy to focus on a specific apparent imperfection in the universe, but it may have great value in God's wider scheme of things. He considers that most of his errors arise through the difference between his intellect, which is finite and error-prone, and his will, which seems to have no limitations. Indeed, God's faculty of willing seems no greater, making the will a reason for believing he is made in God's image. It is no good blaming God for making him free to give or withhold assent in matters about which God has not given him a clear and distinct perception; he must not judge things he does not understand properly.

However, he does not seem entirely satisfied. God could have ensured that he did not make mistakes, without limiting his freedom, or giving him more than finite knowledge, by giving him clear and distinct perceptions in all the matters he thinks about, or made him in such a way that he always applied the rule of not judging things he did not understand clearly and distinctly. He must always apply this rule, and accept that the universe is more perfect (as it contains greater variety) by having some imperfect parts than not, and that his part in it is not a perfect one.

Descartes asks himself (**Meditation Five**) what he can be certain of about material things. Even if they are not external objects, they have properties that are independent of his mind, such as the essence of a triangle, which is to have three angles, equal to two right angles. And, if he can derive the idea of something from thought, and what he clearly and distinctly perceives as belonging to it does, this will give him another proof of God's existence. He has the idea of God, and that always existing belongs to his nature, just as clearly and distinctly as he has any mathematical idea.

Descartes now puts forward his version of the ontological argument for God's existence, first formulated by Anselm in his *Proslogion*. Anselm argued that, as God is that than which nothing greater can be thought, he must exist in reality, as this is greater than existing only in the understanding; and he cannot be thought not to exist, because something that cannot be thought not to exist is greater than something that can be thought not to exist. Understanding that God is that than which nothing greater can be thought is to understand that he exists in such a way that he cannot fail to exist, even in thought. By treating existence as an attribute or perfection, which it is better to possess than not, Anselm considered he had proved both God's existence in reality and his necessary existence, because there is a contradiction involved in thinking that that than which nothing greater can be thought does not exist.

However, Thomas Aquinas rejected Anselm's argument in his *Summa Theologica*. If we knew God's essence, we would know he is a being that must exist; but, not knowing God's essence, if we wish to prove his existence, we need to use [*a posteriori*] arguments and start, not with God, but with what we know, the world God has made, and argue from it to God. But the ontological argument continued to fascinate philosophers like Descartes. He begins by noting that, as existence can be distinguished from essence in everything else, this must also be the case with God, who can be thought of as not existing. However, careful consideration shows that existence can no more be separated from God's essence than its having three angles that are equal to two right angles can from the essence of a triangle. As God is supremely perfect, it is contradictory to think that he lacks the perfection of existence. So Descartes treats existence explicitly as one of

8

the perfections that a supremely perfect being must possess.

Descartes himself wonders whether it can be this simple. Although he cannot, for example, think of a mountain without a valley, this does not mean that a mountain or valley actually exist; only that, whether or not they do, they cannot be separated from each other. However, he maintains that this sort of consideration does not apply to God. From the fact that he cannot think of God, except as existing, it follows that existence is inseparable from him, and so he really exists. And it is not that his thought imposes this necessity; it is the necessity of God's existence that compels him to think it. He might never think about God but, if he does, must ascribe every perfection to him. As existence is one, he is right to conclude that God exists. It is to God's essence alone that existence belongs, and there could not be more than one such God.

Descartes insists that one of the problems, when thinking about God, is that our prejudices, and particularly the priority we give to sense experience, prevent our seeing what should be obvious – that he exists and that this belongs to his essence alone. However, a nagging doubt remains. The problem (he says) is that, although he believes this argument to be true, while he clearly and distinctly perceives it, he is not always concentrating on it, so, if he were ignorant of God, he might, on hearing counter-arguments, start to doubt what he had clearly perceived.

If Descartes had been around 140 years later, he would have seen that lapses of concentration are not the only problem. The fundamental criticism of the ontological argument was made by Immanuel Kant in his *Critique of Pure Reason* (Book II, Chapter III, Section IV), published in 1781. Kant directs his fire specifically at Descartes' version of the argument, arguing that it confuses logical necessity and necessary existence.

If we suppose that a triangle exists, three angles must necessarily exist in it, because having three angles is part of the definition of a triangle: it is self-contradictory to suppose the existence of the triangle, but not its three angles. However, it is not self-contradictory to suppose the non-existence of the triangle with its angles. Similarly, if we form an *a priori* concept of God that includes existence, it will be self-contradictory to deny he exists. But there is no contradiction if both God and existence (subject and predicate) are suppressed, for then: 'there is *nothing* at all . . . Annihilate its existence in thought, and you annihilate the thing itself with all its predicates; how then can there be any room for contradiction?' If we build existence into our concept of God, denying his existence is self-contradictory; and, in this sense, he cannot be thought not to exist. But this does not prove that God actually exists.

However, Kant's criticism of the ontological argument goes further: that it wrongly treats existence as a perfection. Existence is not a concept of something that can be added to the concept of a thing. To say, 'God is', adds no new predicate to the concept of God, but just affirms the existence of the subject, God, with all its predicates. A hundred real pounds contains no more money than a hundred possible pounds. If they did, the concept would not correspond exactly to its object. Therefore, whatever the number of predicates, by which we think a thing, nothing is added to the object of the concept by the statement that the thing exists. If it were: 'not exactly the same, but something more than what was thought in my concept, would exist'.

Thus, existence is not (as Descartes claims) a perfection that something has. To say that something exists is to say that there exists in reality an object that corresponds to our concept. The Christian concept of God is of an infinite being and, if he exists, he exists in a completely different way from everything else because, unlike everything else, which he has created from nothing, he exists through himself. But such a being can be thought not to exist, and there is no contradiction involved in doing so.

However, Descartes regards his argument as satisfactory. As he knows that God is no deceiver, and has concluded that what he sees clearly and distinctly is necessarily true, no counter-argument can make him doubt it. He now knows how to determine truth – anything that is evident to his intellect is entirely true. Truth and certainty in everything depend on knowledge of God, and he is now in a position to achieve certain knowledge of many things.

Descartes now knows (**Meditation Six**) that material things exist as objects of pure mathematics, because he clearly and distinctly perceives this to be the case. But do physical things exist? He wonders if he can base an argument for their existence on sense perception. He used to believe that there were external objects, which were different from his thoughts, and from which his ideas of them came. The ideas did not seem to come from him, because they were more vivid than those in his memory and he could not stop them coming. What had undermined his faith in his senses had been that they misled him; the issue of dreams; and (most serious of all) his ignorance of God, making him think that perceptions, which appeared to come from external objects, might be produced internally. However, now he knows himself and God better, although he will avoid hasty conclusions about sense experience, he will not doubt all of it.

He knows that he exists, and that the only thing that belongs to his essence is that he is a thinking thing. He is also aware that he has a passive faculty of sensing, which receives the ideas of sensible things, but he would not be able to use it without an active faculty, which produces the ideas; and this cannot be inside him, because he has no control over production of the ideas he receives. There are three possibilities as to the source of these ideas: external objects, God or some other creature. As God does not deceive, he does not send them himself, or via another creature; and, as he has strongly inclined Descartes to believe they come from external objects, they must do so. Indeed, there is no reason to doubt what nature teaches, as it is nothing other than the ordered network of things, established by God, so he can accept that there is one particular body that belongs to him; that his body, and his essential, thinking self, form one unit among many; and that he is affected (sometimes painfully) by interaction with these. The point he must always keep in mind is that, although sense perceptions are generally reliable guides to external things, they can give confused information, while it is only from intellectual enquiry, not sense perceptions themselves, that he will learn anything about external objects.

It is also important not to forget that mind and body are completely different – the body is divisible into parts (and mortal), whereas the mind is indivisible (and immortal). Further, the way the mind receives information via the body and brain can (because of the latter's limitations) be misleading. Thus, despite God's goodness, human beings, who consist of distinct minds and bodies, are bound to make mistakes, and must always make full use of all their faculties to try to avoid them. However, as he now knows that God is no deceiver, he can dismiss all his extreme doubts.

In his quest for certainty, Descartes addresses a whole series of fundamental philosophical questions in the *Meditations*: What do we know? How do we know what we know?

Some Issues to Consider

Is it possible to doubt everything? Is there anything of which we can be absolutely certain? What is the nature of the human mind? Does God exist, and can we prove he exists? Is the soul immortal?; and offers answers to them. Although not everyone accepts these answers, it is not surprising that the *Meditations* continue to be essential reading for any student of philosophy.

Some Issues to Consider

- Descartes wants to find something absolutely certain, which will provide a secure basis for all knowledge.
- He believes that philosophers must prove God's existence and the immortality of the soul, because non-believers will not accept what God has revealed in the Bible.
- Descartes believes that an essential prerequisite of proving the immortality of the soul is to establish that it is completely distinct from the body.
- He holds that the soul is pure substance and indivisible, is unaffected by bodily death, and so is immortal.
- Cartesian doubt is a comprehensive doubt that embraces everything that can possibly be doubted, including the existence of the external world.
- Descartes thinks that, because the senses sometimes mislead us, they may always do so, but is this a reasonable position to adopt?
- Descartes decides to conduct himself as if an evil demon were deceiving him, treating external objects as illusions, and regarding himself as without body or senses.
- Descartes holds that the one thing he can be certain of is that he is thinking, and that he is a thinking thing.

Context

- For Descartes, knowledge starts with the mind and thought (rationalism), not sense experience (empiricism).
- He maintains that his realization that wax can change (when heated) comes through mental inspection and judgement, not the senses.
- He considers he can take it as a general rule that what he clearly and distinctly perceives is true.
- Descartes argues that, as an effect cannot be more perfect than its cause, his idea of an infinite being cannot have originated in his own mind, as he is finite, and so must have come from an infinite being. Does this prove that God exists?
- His awareness of his own defects makes him realize that he is dependent on a thinking thing, God, who possesses all perfections, and who is his sole cause and preserver.
- Descartes argues that human beings' finite minds are unable to understand why God did not make them incapable of error, and that what appears to be an imperfection in the universe may have great value in God's wider scheme of things.
- Descartes maintains that existence can no more be separated from God's essence than its having three angles, equal to a right angle, can from the essence of a triangle.
- Are Kant's criticisms of the ontological argument convincing?
- Once Descartes understands what he is himself (a thinking thing), and realizes that God is not a deceiver, he decides that he need not doubt the whole of sense experience.
- Descartes concludes that God does not send sense experiences himself, nor via another creature and, as he has strongly inclined human beings to believe they come from external objects, they must do so.
- Despite God's goodness, as human beings consist of dis-

tinct minds and bodies, they are bound to make mistakes, and Descartes warns that they must always make full use of all their faculties to try to avoid them; however, there is no need for extreme doubt.

Suggestions for Further Reading

R. Descartes, *Discourse on Method and Meditations on First Philosophy*, trans. D. A. Cress, fourth edition, Indianapolis/Cambridge: Hackett Publishing Company, 1998.

R. Descartes, *Meditations, Objections and Replies*, eds R. Ariew and D. A. Cress, Indianapolis/Cambridge: Hackett Publishing Company, 2006.

Anselm, Proslogion with the Replies of Gaunilo and Anselm, ed. T. Williams, Indianapolis/Cambridge: Hackett Publishing Company, 2001.

Basic Writings of Saint Thomas Aquinas, vol. I, ed. A. C. Pegis, Indianapolis/Cambridge: Hackett Publishing Company, 1997.

J. Cottingham, *Descartes*, Oxford and Malden MA: Blackwell Publishers, 1986.

J. Cottingham, *The Rationalists*, A History of Western Philosophy, vol. 4, Oxford and New York: Oxford University Press, 1988.

G. Hatfield, *Routledge Philosophy Guidebook to Descartes and the Meditations*, London and New York: Routledge, 2003.

I. Kant, *Critique of Pure Reason*, ed. V. Politis, London: Everyman, 1993.

A. Kenny, *Descartes: A Study of His Philosophy*, New York: Random House, 1968.

T. Sorrell, *Descartes*, Oxford and New York: Oxford University Press, 1987.

Detailed Summary of René Descartes' *Meditations on First Philosophy*

To those Most Wise and Distinguished Men, the Dean and Doctors of the Faculty of Sacred Theology of Paris (pp. 47–50)

René Descartes Sends Greetings

I am sure that, once you have understood what this work is about, you will wish to defend it.

I have always thought the two issues of '**God** and the **soul**' to be among those that **philosophy**, rather than **theology**, ought to **demonstrate** because, although believers accept through **faith** that the soul does not die, **only 'natural reason' can convince non-believers of religious truths** (p. 47). We should, of course, believe in God on the basis of 'the **Holy Scriptures**', and believe in them because they 'come from God', but this kind of argument will not persuade unbelievers (p. 47). And, indeed, all **theologians** maintain that **God's existence** can be proved philosophically, while there is ample scriptural support for the view that it is 'easier' to achieve knowledge of God than of '**creatures**' (p. 47). Thus, it is appropriate to enquire how we may know God 'more easily and with greater certainty than the things of this world' (p. 47).

Some have argued that little can be known of the soul, and that only faith can assure us of its **immortality**. But 'the **Lateran Council** held under **Leo X**' urged philosophers to refute this argument (p. 48). Further, many doubt God's existence, and deny that mind and body are distinct, because no one has proved 'these two things' (p. 48). However, I believe that the arguments for God and the soul have, if fully understood, 'the force of a demonstration', and that there is no more important task for the **philosopher** than to identify the best of these arguments, and present them 'precisely and plainly' (p. 48).

This 'treatise' contains the main arguments on these subjects, and no human mind could find 'better ones' (p. 48). However, as with proofs in **geometry**, not every mind is sufficiently unprejudiced, or capable of rising above that which is associated 'with the **senses**', to be able to grasp them. Certainly, the world contains no more people with a greater 'aptitude for **metaphysical studies**' than for geometry (p. 49). Also, people have a tendency to try to appear clever by 'arrogantly challenging' even the best philosophical arguments (p. 49).

So, even though I have assembled the best arguments, I do not think that I shall achieve my purpose without the **Sorbonne**'s support, as it is so highly esteemed in matters of faith and '**human philosophy**' (p. 49). I would be grateful if you would correct any errors in my work, and then endorse it. If my arguments can be made sufficiently lucid to be seen as precise demonstrations of God's existence and that mind and body are distinct, this will ensure that all errors about these matters are 'erased' from men's minds (pp. 49–50). Your endorsement will probably cause even **atheists** to 'put aside their **spirit of contrariness**' (p. 50). And you are better equipped than anybody to judge how useful this would be to 'the **cause of God and religion**' (p. 50).

Preface to the Reader (pp. 51–3)

I dealt with God and the human mind in my *Discourse on Method*, but I did not discuss them at length in a book written in French, in case it led 'weaker minds' to think they could understand these questions (p. 51). But I did invite readers to inform me of any objections they had. Two are worthy of note.

First, it does not follow from the fact that the mind, when turned upon itself, perceives itself to be a **'thinking thing'** that its *'essence'* is only this, excluding 'everything else' that might belong to the **'nature of the soul'** (p. 51). My point was that I was aware of nothing that 'I knew belonged to my essence', apart from being a 'thinking thing' (p. 51). However, I will show that it follows from this that 'nothing else really does belong to it' (p. 51). Second, it does not follow from my having 'an **idea** of a thing more **perfect** than me' that the idea is more perfect, or that what it represents exists (p. 51). But there is an ambiguity in the word 'idea', which can be interpreted as referring to the 'operation' of my intellect, or to what is 'represented' by that operation (p. 51). And the latter, even if it is considered not to exist **'outside the intellect'**, can, by its essence, be 'more perfect than me' (p. 51). I will explain below how it follows from there being within me 'an idea of something more perfect than me' that 'this thing really exists' (pp. 51–2).

Two **'treatises'**, based on 'atheist' arguments, attacked my conclusions, but I shall not waste time responding to them (p. 52). Atheist arguments usually involve **'ascribing human emotions to God'**, or arrogant claims that **'finite'** human minds can fully understand what an **'incomprehensible and infinite'** God 'can and ought to do' (p. 52).

What follows deals with the questions of God and the human mind, together with the 'starting points of the whole of **first philosophy**' (p. 52). It should be read only by those few people who are prepared to think seriously about such matters, and withdraw their minds from 'the senses as well as from all **prejudices**' (p. 52). I shall set out the thoughts that have led me to 'a **certain and evident knowledge of the truth**', to establish whether they can convince others (p. 52). Then I shall reply to objections raised by those 'learned gentlemen', who read the work before publication; and I urge readers not to 'form a judgment' about my *Meditations* until they have read both the objections and my replies (pp. 52–3).

Synopsis of the Following Six Meditations (pp. 54–6)

The **First Meditation** deals with 'why we can doubt all things' (p. 54). The 'utility' of such an **'extensive' doubt** is to remove prejudices, 'withdraw the mind from the senses', and to make it impossible for us to doubt things 'we later discover to be true' (p. 54). In the **Second Meditation**, the mind 'supposes the nonexistence of all those things' it can doubt, enabling it to distinguish between what belongs 'to an **intellectual nature**' and 'the body' (p. 54). It does not contain proof of 'the immortality of the soul', but of an essential '**prerequisite**' of doing so: a 'lucid' concept of the soul as 'utterly distinct from every concept of a body' (p. 54). We can understand a body only as '**divisible**', but the mind only as 'indivisible' (p. 54). So, the decay of the body does not mean '**annihilation**' **of the mind** (p. 55). The mind does not consist of '**accidents**'; it is '**pure substance**' so, while the body can 'easily perish', the mind is 'immortal' (p. 55). The **Third Meditation** contains my '**principal argument**' **for God's existence**, and shows why our idea of a '**supremely perfect being**' has such '**objective reality**' that it 'can only come from a **supremely perfect cause**' (p. 55).

The **Fourth Meditation** proves that everything we 'clearly and distinctly perceive' is true; and the 'nature of falsity' is also explained (p. 55).

In the **Fifth Meditation**, '**corporeal nature**' is explained, and there is a further proof of God's existence (p. 56). The **Sixth Meditation** distinguishes the 'understanding' from the '**imagination**', and proves that the mind is distinct from the body, even though it 'forms a single unit with it' (p. 56). The errors arising from 'the senses' (and how to avoid them) are set out (p. 56). There is also consideration of the arguments from which we 'infer the existence of **material things**', which shows that they are less 'firm' than those which lead us to 'knowledge of our mind and of God': the 'most certain' thing that we can know (p. 56).

Meditations on First Philosophy in which the Existence of God and the Distinction Between the Soul and the Body Are Demonstrated

Meditation One: Concerning those Things that Can Be Called Into Doubt (pp. 59–63)

Several years ago, I realized that I had regarded many 'false opinions' as true, making everything based on them 'doubtful'; and that, to be certain of anything, I needed to start again from the 'original foundations' (p. 59). I put this 'enormous' task off for a long time, but have now decided to begin 'general demolition of my opinions' (p. 59). I must 'withhold' assent from any uncertain and doubtful ones, as well as from those that are '**patently false**' (p. 59). I do not need to examine every opinion 'individually'; it will be enough to tackle 'those principles' that underpin all my beliefs (pp. 59–60).

The beliefs I regard as 'most true' come through the **senses**, but they can deceive us, making it prudent not to trust them completely (p. 60). But are there not some things that it is impossible to doubt, such as my sitting here now? How could I doubt that these are my hands and body – unless I am mad, and I would be mad to base my behaviour on those who are.

But, I dream about all sorts of things, such as being here when, in fact, I am asleep in bed. However, would my awareness that I am stretching out my hand be so 'distinct', if I were asleep (p. 60)? Then again, there are no 'definitive signs' by which to 'distinguish being awake from being asleep' (p. 60).

Let me assume that I am dreaming. Surely, the things I see could 'only have been produced in the likeness of true things' (pp. 60–1). Indeed, when painters depict imaginary creatures with 'bizarre forms', they just put together the parts of actual animals in a new way (p. 61). It is from things in the real world that we create things in thought. Things that are '**simple** and **universal**', such as 'corporeal nature' and '**extension**' therefore seem to be true (p. 61). Perhaps, we can conclude that those disciplines, such as physics and medicine, which involve '**composite** things', are doubtful, but those involving the 'simplest and most general things', such as arithmetic and geometry, have a measure of certainty (p. 61). Asleep or awake, 'two plus three make five' (p. 61).

However, what if there is a God, 'able to do anything', who has so arranged matters that there is 'no earth' or anything else, but things still 'appear to me to exist precisely as they do now' (p. 61). Indeed, I may be deceived, even when 'I add two and three' (p. 61). God is said to be '**supremely good**', so perhaps he has not '**willed**' that I be deceived' all the time; but why then am I deceived 'occasionally' (pp. 61–2)?

Some would rather deny 'so **powerful** a God' than believe everything else to be 'uncertain' (p. 62). However, the less powerful the 'author of my origin', the more likely it is that I am 'imperfect' and 'always deceived' (p. 62). It seems 'permissible' to doubt all my former beliefs, so I must 'withhold assent' even from them, if I am to be 'certain' of anything (p. 62).

However, 'long-standing opinions' are difficult to discard, particularly if, though doubtful, they still seem 'highly probable' (p. 62). Therefore, I must treat them all as 'wholly false and imaginary', so that nothing will prevent me from gaining the correct view of things (p. 62). Instead of a 'supremely good God', I will believe that an **'evil genius'** is using all his power and skill to deceive me (p. 62). I will regard all apparently **'external things'**, such as heaven and earth, as **'bedeviling hoaxes'**, and think of myself as without physical **attributes** or senses, but as 'falsely believing' that I have them (p. 62). This will ensure that I withhold assent from anything false, and prevent the 'deceiver' tricking me (pp. 62–3). But doing so is 'arduous'; and I am inclined to return to my 'old opinions' (p. 63).

Meditation Two: Concerning the Nature of the Human Mind: That It Is Better Known than the Body (pp. 63–9)

I shall return to the 'path' I was on yesterday, treating everything doubtful as 'completely false', until I find 'something certain', or conclude that nothing is (p. 63). Supposing 'everything I see is false', what is true (p. 63)? Perhaps only 'the single fact that nothing is certain' (p. 63).

But is there something about which there is no doubt? Is there not a God, who gives me these thoughts? But I myself may be their 'author' (p. 63). So, I am 'at least something' (p. 63). I have denied that I have a body or senses, and convinced myself that there is no external world. Do I 'not exist' then (p. 64)? But I do exist, 'if I persuaded myself of something' (p. 64). Even if there is a 'supremely powerful' and cunning deceiver, I exist, if he is deceiving me; I am not nothing while I think that 'I am something' (p. 64). So, this statement, '"I am, I exist" is **necessarily true**' on every occasion that I say or think it (p. 64).

But, what am I? I must take care not to be mistaken about the very piece of knowledge I regard as 'the most certain and evident of all' (p. 64). Previously, I thought of myself as a man, or '**rational animal**', but this raises questions about the meaning of these terms (p. 64). So, what came 'spontaneously' into my thoughts when I reflected on 'what I was' (p. 64)? My first thought used to be that I had a body, and I believed I 'knew its nature distinctly' (p. 64). But what am I now, with an all-powerful '**malicious deceiver**' trying to trick me (p. 65)? Nothing relating to the body comes to mind, but what about 'thinking' (p. 65)? It exists, and 'cannot be separated from me' (p. 65). As long as I am thinking, I exist, for if I stopped thinking, I would 'cease to exist' (p. 65). So, I am 'nothing but a thinking thing', a mind or **reason** (p. 65).

Am I anything else? I shall use 'my imagination' (p. 65). I am not just a 'human body', nor 'anything I devise for myself' (p. 65). But, I am 'something', and I know 'I exist' (p. 65). So who is 'this "I"' (p. 65)? It does not depend on things I do not know, nor on things in my imagination. I must be careful to detach my mind from such things, so that 'it can perceive its nature as distinctly as possible' (p. 66). So what am I? A 'thing that thinks', which includes doubting, understanding, affirming, imagining and sensing (p. 66).

Indeed, I am the one who, at this moment, doubts 'almost everything', but who still 'understands something' and observes 'many things' that seem to come from the senses (p. 66). Even if God is deceiving me, which of these things is not 'every bit as true as the fact that I exist' (p. 66)? Clearly, I am the one doubting, understanding and imagining, and these are 'part of my thought'; and I am the one who is aware of physical things 'as if through the senses' (p. 66).

But I still cannot help thinking that 'corporeal things' are known 'more distinctly' than this 'I' (p. 66). But it would be very odd to understand the things I doubt better than myself. The problem is that my mind does not wish to be 'restricted within the confines of truth' (p. 67).

Let us think about the things we seem to understand very fully: 'the bodies we touch and see' (p. 67). This 'piece of wax' is 'hard and cold', and 'easy to touch'; it seems to have all the characteristics required to enable it to be known 'distinctly' (p. 67). However, I am now holding it near to the fire. It is becoming 'liquid and hot' and difficult to touch (p. 67). Is it the same piece of wax? Nobody says it is not, but none of the characteristics that enabled it to be known distinctly now remain.

Perhaps, the wax showed itself in one way, and now does so in another. So, what is left after removing everything not belonging to the wax? Only something that is 'extended, flexible and **mutable**' (p. 67). Of course, I understand that the wax can undergo 'innumerable changes', but I do not do so through my imagination: 'I perceive it through the mind alone' (pp. 67–8). What I need to realize is that, despite appearances to the contrary, my '**perception**' of the wax is not to do with seeing, touching or imagining (p. 68). It is an 'inspection' by the 'mind alone' (p. 68).

But how liable my mind is to be mistaken, not least because of the way we talk about things. We say that we 'see the wax itself', not that we 'judge it to be present from its color or shape' (p. 68). This suggests knowledge of the wax through seeing rather than mental inspection. What I thought I knew through seeing, in fact I understood with 'the **faculty of judgment**, which is in my mind' (p. 68). How, therefore, did I see what the piece of wax really was? It was with my mind that I distinguished 'the wax from its external forms', and saw it 'in its nakedness' (pp. 68–9).

But, on this basis, what can I now say about 'this mind', about 'myself' (p. 69)? However I judge that the wax exists (whether through touching, or imagining it), it cannot be the case that, while I do so, 'I who think am not something' (p. 69). And everything that assists my perception of the wax, or 'any other body', makes even clearer 'the nature of my mind' (p. 69). Now I know that even physical things are not 'perceived by the senses', but by 'the intellect alone'; so, there is nothing that I can perceive with less difficulty 'than my own mind' (p. 69).

Meditation Three: Concerning God, that He Exists (pp. 69–81)

Now I shall eliminate all '**images** of corporeal things' from my thoughts or, at least, treat them as 'empty, false and worthless' (pp. 69–70). This will help me to know myself better. I am 'a thing that thinks', and even if the things I 'sense or imagine' do not exist 'outside me', the '**modes of thinking**' that relate to them 'exist within me' (p. 70). This is what I 'truly know' (p. 70). But do I know what I require to be 'certain of anything' (p. 70)? In this first piece of knowledge, there is nothing but a '**clear and distinct perception** of what I affirm'. However, I would not be certain of anything, if something I clearly perceived could prove 'false' (p. 70). So, I can take it as a 'general rule' that what I see 'clearly and distinctly' is true (p. 70).

But I have acknowledged as 'certain and evident' things I later found to be 'doubtful', such as all the things perceived through 'the senses' (p. 70). I know that I have the 'ideas' of these things, but I used to think, mistakenly, that I 'clearly perceived' that the things, from which these ideas 'proceeded', existed 'outside me' (p. 70). But surely, when it comes to something as basic as two plus three making five, I do '**intuit**' this clearly enough to be able to 'affirm' it as true (p. 70). Admittedly, I did decide to doubt such things, but only because I thought God might be deceiving me. When I think of God's 'supreme power', I am forced to accept that he could easily mislead me, even in matters that seem clear to my mind (p. 71). Yet, I am so convinced by such things that I say to myself: as long as I think 'I am something, he will never bring it about that I am nothing', for now 'I do exist' (p. 71). And God cannot make two plus three not add up to five, because that would be an 'obvious **contradiction**' (p. 71). Further, as I have no evidence of God being 'a deceiver' (or even existing), my doubting God rests on a '**tenuous**' and '**metaphysical**' hypothesis (p. 71). So, I need to ask whether God exists and whether or not he can deceive; I can be 'certain' of nothing, unless I answer these questions (p. 71).

But first, I must put my thoughts, which are of different kinds, into their respective 'classes', to determine which are true and false (p. 71). Some thoughts are 'ideas', or 'images of things', as of the sky or God (p. 71). On the other hand, when 'I will', or 'affirm', something, there is more in the thought than the 'likeness' of the thing: some are '**volitions**', others 'judgments' (p. 71). Considered in isolation, these 'ideas' cannot be false (p. 71). Whatever I imagine, I am definitely imagining it, and, even if I choose '**evil**' or 'non-existent' things, I am still choosing them (p. 71). Now, when judging, my 'most frequent error' is to judge that the ideas I have conform with 'things outside me' (pp. 71–2). But, there can be no error, if I regard them 'merely as certain modes of my thought' (p. 72). These ideas differ. Some seem '**innate**', while others seem to come from external sources (p. 72). Why do I think this? Because '**nature**' has taught me so, and, as when I feel heat, they do not seem to 'depend upon my will' (p. 72).

But are these good enough reasons? The fact that I have a **natural 'impulse'** to believe that some ideas come from external sources does not mean they do; indeed, following natural impulses has often led to poor choices (p. 72). The fact that these ideas come independently of my will does not 'necessarily' mean they come from things 'outside me'; they may be produced from within, like the ideas I have when sleeping (p. 72). Then, even if these ideas come from outside sources, it does not 'follow' that they resemble them (p. 73). The sun appears to be 'quite small', but '**astronomical reasoning**' shows it is larger than the earth; and both ideas cannot resemble the sun outside me (p. 73). This indicates an insecure basis for my belief that external things send me ideas through the 'sense organs' (p. 73).

I can approach the question from a different angle. Ideas, which involve '**substances**', have more 'objective reality' than those representing 'modes or accidents', while the idea of a '**supreme deity**', who is '**eternal, infinite, omniscient, omnipotent**', and who made everything apart from himself, is more objectively real than those relating to '**finite substances**' (p. 73). Now, an '**effect**' gets its reality from its '**cause**', and the latter could not do so, unless it had 'that reality' (p. 73). Something cannot 'come into being' from nothing, nor can what is 'less perfect' give rise to something 'more perfect' (p. 73). So, the idea of, for example, heat, must be put into me by a cause that has at least as much '**formal reality**' as there is 'objective reality' in the idea of it (p. 74). If the idea contained something not in the cause, it would be getting 'something from nothing' (p. 74).

Further, although it is 'objective reality' that I am considering 'in my ideas', that does not mean I should conclude that 'the same reality' does not need to be 'formally' in their causes (p. 74). Although one idea can 'issue' from another, there cannot be an '**infinite regress**': there must be a 'first idea', with a cause that is the '**archetype**', containing 'formally all the reality', which is in the idea 'merely objectively' (p. 74). Clearly, the ideas I have are 'like **images**': they may not equal, but cannot exceed, the 'perfection' of the things from which they derive (p. 74). So what is my conclusion? If I am convinced that the 'objective reality' of an idea is too 'great' to have originated in me, it 'necessarily follows that I am not alone in the world'. But if I am not, I cannot be certain that anything other than myself exists (p. 74).

In addition to my idea of myself, my ideas include those of, for example, God, 'corporeal things', animals and 'other men' (p. 75). I might have 'fashioned' my ideas of men and animals from those I have of God, myself and corporeal things (p. 75). With the last-mentioned idea, there is nothing 'so great' about it that it could not have started in me (p. 75). It has only a few clear and distinct characteristics, such as size, length, breadth, substance and so on. As to such features as light, colour and 'heat and cold', they are so 'confused' that my ideas of them may be of 'non-things' (p. 75). For example, is cold 'privation of heat', or is it the other way round (p. 75)? If the former, my idea that cold is 'real and positive' is 'false' (p. 75). And I could have taken an idea, such as substance, from my 'idea of myself' (pp. 75–6). I think of myself as a 'thinking', not an 'extended' thing, whereas the opposite is true of a stone; but, though so different, both seem to be substances (p. 76).

But could my idea of God have started in me? I think of God as an 'infinite' and 'supremely powerful' 'substance', who **created** me and all that exists, if 'anything else' does (p. 76). Now, although I have the idea of substance, because 'I am a substance', I am 'finite', so this does not account for my idea of **'infinite substance'** (p. 76). As the idea must have come from an infinite substance, 'I must conclude that **God necessarily exists**' (p. 76). And there seems to be 'more reality' in infinite, than in finite, substance (p. 76). Indeed, 'perception of God' is prior to that of myself, and I see my own **'defects'** through having the idea of a 'more perfect being' (p. 76). As the 'most clear and distinct' idea, it is the least likely to be false (p. 77). I could pretend that 'such a being' does not exist, but not that the idea of this being indicates 'nothing real' (p. 77). All that I recognize as involving some perfection is 'wholly contained' in this idea (p. 77). My not understanding the infinite is beside the point, because such understanding is not attainable by one who is 'finite' (p. 77). So, my idea of God is the 'most true, the most clear and distinct' that I have (p. 77).

However, **'potentially'** I could have the **'perfections'** I ascribe to God (p. 77). My 'knowledge' is increasing, and could reach **'infinity'**; and, if I have such potential, why should it not give rise to 'the idea of these perfections' (p. 77)? But, there is nothing potential in God, so my knowledge's 'gradual increase' proves my 'imperfection', while his being 'actually infinite' means his 'perfection' cannot be added to (p. 77).

The problem is that when my mind is overwhelmed by '**sensible things**', I overlook the fact that the idea of a being 'more perfect than me' must come from one who actually is so (p. 78).

What, then, is the 'source' of my existence (p. 78)? If I 'got my being' from myself, I would 'be God', and would have endowed myself with 'all the perfections' that are 'contained in the idea of God', none of which would have been harder to acquire than for me, a 'substance that thinks', to '**emerge out of nothing**' (p. 78).

I could suppose that 'I have always existed' (p. 78). Would that remove the need for an '**author of my existence**' (p. 78)? But, it does not follow, from my existing a short time ago, that 'I must exist now', unless there is some **preserving 'cause'** (p. 78). The same 'force and action' are needed to 'preserve', as to 'create', something (p. 78). Do I have the power to ensure my continued existence? As a 'thinking thing', I would be aware of it. I do not have it, and so must 'depend upon some other being than myself' (p. 79).

But I could have been 'produced' by my parents, or some cause 'less perfect than God' (p. 79). However, the cause cannot be inferior to 'the effect' (p. 79). As a thinking thing with a 'certain idea of God', my cause must be a thinking thing with 'an idea of all the perfections' I ascribe to God (p. 79). Now, if this cause received its existence 'from itself', clearly it is God because, with the '**power of existing in and of itself**', it possesses all the perfections I ascribe to God (p. 79). If its existence came from 'another cause', I shall continue my enquiry until I reach 'the **ultimate cause**': God (p. 79). There can no 'infinite regress', as I am concerned with that cause that produced and which preserves me (p. 79). It cannot be the case that '**several partial causes**' have combined to produce me (p. 79). One of the 'chief perfections' that I understand God to possess is his '**unity**' and 'simplicity' (p. 79).

What about my parents? They do not preserve me, nor could they have made me 'a thinking thing' (p. 80). They only affected the '**matter**', which contains me, 'a mind' (p. 80). Therefore, the fact that I exist, and have 'an idea of a most perfect being', shows that God exists (p. 80). So where did I get 'this idea of God' from (p. 80)? It did not come 'from the senses', nor did I make it; it must be 'innate' (p. 80). And, it is not surprising that God gave me this idea. As God has made me, it is all the more credible that he should have done so 'in his **image and likeness**', and that I see this likeness with 'the same **faculty** by which I perceive myself' (p. 80). So, when I think about myself, I recognize myself as 'incomplete' and 'dependent' upon a being, who possesses, 'infinitely and actually', all the greater and better things to which I aspire (p. 80). It would be 'impossible for me to exist', and have 'the idea of God', unless God existed; and, as deception springs from a 'defect', of which God has none, clearly he is no 'deceiver' (p. 80).

But now I must contemplate God and his 'attributes' as closely as my limited powers permit, as doing so gives 'the greatest pleasure' attainable in this life (pp. 80–1).

Meditation Four: Concerning the True and the False (pp. 81–7)

While 'withdrawing my mind from the senses', I have noticed how many more things are 'truly perceived' about the mind than physical things (p. 81). When I focus on myself as an 'incomplete and dependent' thing, I have a 'clear and distinct' idea of God (p. 81). And, from the fact that I exist with this idea, I conclude that God, on whom my existence depends, 'also exists' (p. 81).

I now see a way to move on to 'knowledge of other things' (p. 81). First, God, who has no 'imperfection', does not deceive me (p. 81). Further, I have a God-given 'faculty of judgment', which will not mislead me if 'I use it properly' (p. 81).

However, it seems to follow that I should be 'incapable' of error (p. 81). Now, when thinking about God, I am, but I make 'countless errors' when I go back to thinking about myself (pp. 81–2). I believe that I have been 'constituted' as a **'middle ground' between 'the supreme being and non-being'** (p. 82). As God's creation, there is no means by which I can be 'led into error' but, through participating to some extent in non-being, I can; I do not have an 'infinite' **faculty of judgement** (p. 82).

However, God could have so made me that 'I never erred', so why did he not do so (p. 82)? Then again, it is not surprising if God, who is **'incomprehensible'** and infinite, does things for reasons 'I do not understand'; and this is certainly no reason for doubting his existence (p. 82). Indeed, when we contemplate 'the **works of God**', we should not concentrate on the apparent imperfection of a part of the universe 'in isolation', but on how it may fit into 'the **universal scheme of things**' (pp. 82–3).

The errors I make arise from 'the simultaneous concurrence of two causes': my faculties of knowing and choosing; that is, 'intellect and will' (p. 83). The intellect just enables me to 'perceive ideas, about which I can render a judgment', and it contains no error when considered thus (p. 83). Of course, there may be 'countless things' about which I do not know, but I cannot prove that God 'ought' to have given me more knowledge than I have (p. 83). My **ability to choose freely** is 'limited by no boundaries', but I can see that, apart from my will, I have no faculty that could not be 'greater' (p. 83).

For example, my 'faculty of understanding' seems 'limited', and I can conceive of an 'infinite' one, which relates to 'the **nature of God**', whose faculties are 'boundless' (p. 83). But, my will is the 'basis' for understanding that I am made in God's 'image and likeness', for God's 'faculty of willing' seems no greater than mine (pp. 83–4). Willing is being able 'to do or not do' something suggested 'by our intellect', such that we sense that no '**external force**' determines our decision (p. 84). This is not to say that I am not free, if I am inclined to one decision rather than another because, through 'divine **grace** or natural knowledge', I recognize 'the good and the true' in it (p. 84). This makes me more free, whereas being indifferent about a decision, because no reason moves me one way or another, reflects a negation of knowledge (p. 84).

It is not my powers of willing and understanding, by themselves, that lead me to make mistakes, but the fact that the will 'extends' beyond 'the intellect', to matters 'I do not understand' (p. 84). It can 'easily' depart from the 'true and the good'; as a result, 'I am deceived and I **sin**' (p. 84). My present examination of whether anything exists 'in the world' illustrates my point (p. 84). I observed that my existence followed from 'the very fact' of my 'making this examination' (p. 84). However, I felt compelled to judge my conclusion to be true, not by an 'external force', but because the 'great light in my intellect gave way to a great inclination of the will' (pp. 84–5).

Anyway, I know that, as a 'certain thinking thing', I exist (p. 85). But are my 'thinking' and 'corporeal' natures different, or 'one and the same thing' (p. 85)? Neither alternative convinces my intellect, and so I am 'indifferent' about whether to 'affirm or deny' either one (p. 85). And this kind of indifference applies not only to things about which my intellect 'knows absolutely nothing', but to all those things about which it lacks clear knowledge, 'when the will is deliberating on them' (p. 85). Thus, I shall use 'my freedom properly', if I reach a judgement only when I see that something is true with 'sufficient clarity and distinctness' (p. 85). And I have no reason to complain about God not having given me greater powers of understanding, as not understanding many things is 'the essence of a finite intellect' (p. 85). Rather, I should thank God 'for what he has bestowed upon me' (p. 85). And I cannot complain that the scope of my will is 'wider' than that of my intellect, for, as it is 'indivisible', nothing could be 'removed from it' (pp. 85–6).

I must not complain that God 'concurs with me' in my mistaken judgements (p. 86). To the extent that they 'depend on God', they are 'true and good', while there is more 'perfection' in my being able to make such judgements than not (p. 86). It is not an 'imperfection' in God to have made me free to 'give or withhold assent' in matters about which he has not given me a 'clear and distinct perception'; but it is one in me to judge things 'I do not properly understand' (p. 86). Of course, God could have ensured that I was never mistaken, without limiting my freedom or giving me more than 'finite knowledge' (p. 86). He could have given me a clear and distinct perception in every matter I consider, or have stamped the rule of not judging anything I do not understand clearly and distinctly so 'firmly upon my **memory**' that I always apply it (p. 86). But, although that might have made me 'more perfect', the 'universe as a whole' may be more perfect with some error-prone parts than none; and I must not complain that God has not given me a 'perfect' part (p. 86). I can 'avoid error' by always applying the rule of not judging unless a matter is clear (p. 86).

So, 'every clear and distinct perception' does not 'come from nothing', and, 'necessarily', God must be its 'author' (p. 87). I shall 'attain truth' only by attending carefully to the things I 'perfectly understand', and separating them from those 'I apprehend more confusedly and more obscurely' (p. 87).

Meditation Five: Concerning the Essence of Material Things, and Again Concerning God, that He Exists (pp. 87–92)

Is there any certainty about 'material things' (p. 87)? Before trying to decide, I should think about my ideas of them, to identify those that are 'distinct' (p. 87). I can imagine things 'quantified in length, breadth and depth' and, as I focus on them, I seem to be 'recalling' what I already knew (p. 87). And, even if they do not exist 'outside me', they cannot be regarded as 'nothing' (p. 88). When I imagine a triangle, even if no such thing exists 'outside my thought', it has an 'essence' that is independent of 'my mind' (p. 88). Its 'three angles are equal to two right angles', and so on; and it has these 'properties', irrespective of what I think (p. 88). It is 'irrelevant' to say that my idea of a triangle came 'through the sense organs', because I can 'demonstrate' the properties of other figures that certainly did not (p. 88). These properties are 'patently true', because I 'know them clearly' (p. 88). And I previously regarded the truths of 'pure and abstract **mathematics**' as the 'most certain of all' (p. 88).

But, if I can elicit the 'idea of something' from thought, and it follows that everything belongs to it that I 'clearly and distinctly' perceive as doing so, this can be used to prove God's existence (p. 88). The idea of God is 'no less within me' than that of any number, and I perceive that his always existing belongs to his 'nature' just as 'clearly and distinctly' (pp. 88–9). So I should be as certain of God's existence as of mathematical truths.

But, with everything else, I am able to distinguish 'existence from essence', so I can persuade myself that this is so with God, too, and that 'he can be thought of as not existing' (p. 89). However, anyone attending carefully to the matter can see that it is no more possible to separate existence 'from God's essence' than to separate its having 'three angles equal to two right angles' from the 'essence of a triangle' (p. 89). It is 'contradictory' to think of God, who is 'supremely perfect', as lacking the 'perfection' of existence (p. 89).

However, I cannot think of a 'mountain without a valley', but this does not mean that there actually is a mountain or valley, only that, 'whether they exist or not', they cannot be separated from each other (p. 89). But, from the fact that 'I cannot think of God except as existing, it follows that existence is inseparable from God', and so he 'really exists' (p. 89). This is not a case of my thought imposing 'any necessity on anything'; it is the 'necessity' of God's existence that compels me to think it (p. 89).

Although I might never happen to think about God, if I do so, I must ascribe all 'perfections' to him, the 'first and supreme' being (p. 90). And, as 'existence is a perfection', I 'rightly conclude that a first and supreme being exists' (p. 90). There are many ways of understanding that this idea is no 'invention', but 'an image of a true and **immutable** nature'. It is to God's essence alone that 'existence belongs'; there could not be more than one such God; I see clearly the necessity of his having existed from, and enduring for, 'eternity'; and God has 'many other features' that I cannot 'remove or change' (p. 90).

I come back to the point that I am only 'fully' convinced by things I perceive 'clearly and distinctly' (p. 90). Some of these things are fairly obvious, while others require careful enquiry but, once 'discovered', are regarded as being as 'certain' as the former (p. 90). As for God, it is only my 'prejudices', and the insistent 'images of sensible things' that make it hard to see 'easily' that he exists (p. 91). For what is more obvious than the existence of God, 'to whose essence alone existence belongs' (p. 90)?

One problem I find is that, although I believe that something is true while I 'clearly and distinctly' perceive it, I cannot always concentrate on that thing (p. 91). As a result, were I 'ignorant of God', I might, on hearing contrary arguments, begin to doubt something 'I perceive most evidently' (p. 91). However, once I saw that God is no 'deceiver', I concluded that what I see clearly and distinctly is 'necessarily true'; and no 'counter-argument' can make me doubt it (p. 91). I now know how to determine truth: 'if anything is evident to my intellect, then it is entirely true' (p. 92).

Thus, every science's truth and certainty depends on 'knowledge of the true God, and I can now achieve 'certain knowledge' of many things, including God himself and 'other intellectual matters', and 'corporeal nature' (p. 92).

Meditation Six: Concerning the Existence of Material Things, and the Real Distinction Between Mind and Body (pp. 92–103)

I must now examine whether 'material things exist' (p. 92). I know they exist as objects of 'pure mathematics', because I 'clearly and distinctly perceive' this (p. 92). Again, I can imagine them, and imagination seems to involve applying 'the knowing faculty' to a body 'intimately present to it', and which exists (p. 92).

So what is the difference between imagination and 'pure **intellection**' (p. 92)? If I imagine a triangle, I understand it to be a three-sided figure and also picture it (p. 92). But, if I 'think about a **chiliagon**', I understand it to have a 'thousand sides', but do not picture it (pp. 92–3) Thus, imagining something requires a 'peculiar sort of effort' by the mind, which understanding it does not (p. 93).

The ability to imagine, unlike that of understanding, is not necessary to the 'essence of my mind' (p. 93). I would be 'the same entity I am now' without it (p. 93). When the mind understands something, it 'turns towards itself and looks at one of the ideas that are in it' (p. 93). However, when it imagines something, it turns to the body, and 'intuits' in it something that 'conforms to an idea' that it understands, or the senses perceive (p. 93). This suggests that a body does exist, but I still do not see how it necessarily follows, from my imagination's 'idea of corporeal nature', that 'some body' does exist (p. 93).

But I imagine many things, such as colours and sounds, which seem to have come to my imagination via the senses. Can I base an argument for the 'existence of corporeal things' on perception through the senses (p. 94)? I shall need to examine the matter carefully, determining what things I used to think true because I perceived them through the senses; why I came to doubt them; and what I believe now.

I used to believe that I: had (or was) a body among many others; judged what was bad or good for me through **sensations of 'pain and pleasure'**; became hungry and thirsty; and experienced 'bodily tendencies' to, for example, mirth and sadness (p. 94). Besides their extension, I sensed **bodies'** '**tactile qualities**' and also light, colour and sound, enabling me to distinguish one body from another (p. 94). So, it is not surprising that I sensed things 'manifestly different from my thought' – the bodies from which these ideas came (p. 94). It seemed 'impossible' that the ideas should originate in me, because they were 'more vivid and explicit' than any formed in thought, or found in memory (p. 94). Further, I could not stop them coming to me, and they only did so when an object was 'present' to one of my sense organs; so I concluded that they 'came from other things' (p. 94).

Also, there seemed good reason to believe that one particular body belonged to me. I could not separate myself from it, and was aware of pain and pleasure in parts of it, but not in 'external' bodies' (p. 95). But why should a certain sensation, such as that called 'hunger', alert me to the need to eat (p. 95)? The answer seemed to be that nature had taught me so, and this was 'how things were' (p. 95).

Then experience undermined my 'faith' in the senses, as they were often mistaken (p. 95). For example, things appearing round from a distance seemed square 'at close quarters' (p. 95). Also, what I thought 'I sensed while awake', I also seemed to sense 'while asleep' (p. 95). As I did not believe that the latter came from 'external' things, I began to doubt that the former did (p. 95). Further, being 'ignorant' of God, there was nothing to stop me thinking that I might be mistaken about what appeared 'most true' (p. 95). I began to doubt what nature had taught me, and to think that some 'unknown' faculty in me produced perceptions of what appeared to be objects external to me (pp. 95–6). However, now that I know myself and God better, I shall avoid 'rashly' believing all the information that seems to come from my senses, but without doubting everything (p. 96).

The first thing I know is that God can make all the things 'I clearly and distinctly understand' in the way 'I understand them' (p. 96). So, as I can understand 'one thing without another', I can be certain that they are separate (p. 96). Thus, as 'I know that I exist', and that the only thing belonging to my essence is that 'I am a thinking thing', I know that this is 'my essence' (p. 96). No doubt, I shall soon be able to say that I have a body 'closely joined to me', but I shall also be certain that I am 'distinct' from it and 'can exist without it' (p. 96).

Further, I have 'faculties of imagining and sensing', which I perceive to be 'distinguished from me as modes from a thing', and which could not exist without me, 'a substance endowed with understanding' (p. 96). I also have 'other faculties', such as being able to move from place to place, but these require an 'extended substance', or body (p. 96). Now, I clearly have a 'passive faculty of sensing', which receives 'ideas of sensible things' (pp. 96–7). However, I would be unable to use it, unless there existed an 'active faculty', which produces these ideas (p. 97). It cannot be in me, because I do not control production of the ideas, so it must be in a substance 'different from me': a body, God, or 'some other creature' (p. 97). As God is no 'deceiver', he does not send me these ideas 'by himself', or through another creature's **mediation** (p. 97). Indeed, he has strongly inclined me to believe they come from 'corporeal things', so these exist (p. 97). I may make mistakes about them, but they certainly contain all that I 'clearly and distinctly understand . . . in a general sense' (p. 97).

Of course, many 'doubtful and uncertain' matters remain, such as the issues of light, sound and pain (p. 97). But God's not being a deceiver gives me hope of finding out the truth about them. And no doubt there is truth in what nature teaches, for 'nature' is 'God himself' or the 'ordered network of created things' he established (p. 97).

Nature uses such sensations as pain and hunger to teach me that my body and I form 'one single thing' (p. 98). If they did not, I would perceive my own bodily injury by 'pure intellect', not pain, and would 'understand' that I needed food, not just feel hungry (p. 98). I am also aware of other bodies around mine, and perceive that I (comprising body and mind) am adversely or beneficially affected by them.

I have referred to nature having taught me things, but I am defining nature 'more narrowly' than the 'combination' of everything God has given me, which includes things belonging to the mind (p. 98). Nature teaches us, for example, to avoid things that cause pain, but does not seem to teach us to draw any conclusions from such 'sense perceptions'; this requires intellectual enquiry into 'external' things (p. 99). A star seems the same size as a flame, but my eye has no 'positive tendency' to believe it is larger (p. 99). So, although I use sense perceptions as 'reliable' guides to external bodies, the information they give is obscure and confused (p. 99). Certainly, nature is 'not omniscient'; but, as human beings are 'limited', only 'limited perfection' suits us (p. 99).

Indeed, errors occur even when nature 'impels' us to things, as when a sick person wants food or drink, which would harm them (pp. 99–100). It is hard to accept that such a person received his 'deception-prone nature from God' (p. 100). So, why does God's 'goodness' not prevent nature from being thus 'deceptive' (p. 100)?

A significant point is the 'great difference' between 'mind and body' (pp. 100–1). The body is 'divisible' into parts, whereas the mind is 'indivisible' (pp. 100–1). Such faculties as 'willing' and 'understanding' are not parts of the mind, as it is the one mind that wills or senses (p. 101). Further, the only part of the body that affects the mind is the brain – in particular, the 'small' part where '**common sense**' is located; and when this part of the brain is 'disposed' in a certain way, it 'presents the same thing to the mind', irrespective of what else is going on in the body (p. 101). Again, if I feel a pain in one part of my body, such as my foot, the sensation is conveyed along nerves from the foot to the brain, affecting the mind with 'a sensation of pain' (p. 101). But, as the nerves pass through other parts of the body, if one of the '**intermediate parts**' is struck, the same movement will occur in the brain, and the mind will experience 'the same pain'; and this can be misleading (p. 101). It must be said, of course, that as any 'motion' in the part of the brain 'affecting the mind' gives rise to only the one sensation, it is best that it is pain, which conduces to the health of human beings; and this testifies to God's 'power and goodness' (p. 102). Again, what could be more useful, in general, for maintaining 'our health' than our getting a 'sensation of thirst' when we need a drink, even if it is not helpful in the specific case of someone with **dropsy** (p. 102)?

But, despite God's goodness, given that we consist of 'mind and body', we are bound to make mistakes (p. 102). As an 'identical motion' in the brain always gives rise to an 'identical sensation' in the mind, it is to be expected that the mind should interpret it as pain to the foot, even it is to another bodily part (p. 102). And, even if drinking is bad for someone with dropsy, it is better for our health that a sense of thirst impels us to drink than no.

In general, the senses more often indicate what is true than not. And, to avoid error, I can use my 'memory' and 'intellect' (p. 103). So, I can dismiss my recent extreme doubts. As for distinguishing between being asleep and being awake, memory does not connect things in dreams with 'other actions of life', nor do they happen in predictable ways (p. 103). What I must do is use all my faculties, sense, memory and intellect, to ensure that I accept nothing from any one of them that 'conflicts with the others' (p. 103). As God is no deceiver, I cannot be 'mistaken', if I enquire carefully into things, although lack of time means that we human beings are bound to make mistakes in 'particular things' (p. 103).

Overview

The following section is a chapter-by-chapter overview of René Descartes' *Meditations on First Philosophy*, designed for quick reference to the detailed summary above. Readers may also find this section helpful for revision.

The italicized sub-headings have been included to make the development of the argument easier to follow.

To those Most Wise and Distinguished Men, the Dean and Doctors of the Faculty of Sacred Theology of Paris (pp. 47–50)

Why God's existence and the immortality of the soul must be proved philosophically

Descartes explains that philosophy, rather than theology, should prove God's existence and the immortality of the soul. Although believers accept them on the basis of faith and holy scripture, only philosophical arguments will convince non-believers. Furthermore, the Lateran Council, held under Leo X, urged philosophers to refute the view that little can be known about the soul. Although many people doubt God's existence and that mind and body are distinct, they can be proved, and his treatise contains the best arguments on these subjects. However, he recognizes that prejudice, ignorance or the desire to appear clever, may still lead people to reject them. As the *Meditations on First Philosophy* will refute errors about God's existence and the soul, he seeks the Sorbonne's endorsement of it, in the hope that their great reputation will persuade even atheists to adopt a sensible attitude.

Detailed Summary of Descartes' Meditations

Preface to the Reader (pp. 51–3)

The contents of the Meditations on First Philosophy

Although he dealt with these subjects in his *Discourse on Method*, it was written in French, so he did not go into detail, in case ignorant people thought they could understand the issues. Two objections to his arguments in that book had been worth noting. First, the fact that the mind, when focused upon itself, sees itself as a thinking thing does not mean that its essence is this alone. His point had been that he is aware of nothing else that belongs to its essence; and he will show that nothing else does. Second, that it does not follow from his having an idea of a thing more perfect than himself that the idea is more perfect, or that what it represents exists. However, the word 'idea' can refer to the operation of the intellect, or to what that operation represents. Even if the latter is thought not to exist outside the intellect, it can, by its essence, be more perfect than him. He will explain how it follows from his having an idea of something more perfect than him that this thing really does exist.

Atheist challenges

Two atheist treatises had challenged his arguments, but did not merit a response. Atheist arguments attributed human emotions to God, or arrogantly claimed that finite human minds can understand an infinite God. As his book deals with the fundamental philosophical questions of God and the human mind, only those willing to approach the issues seriously, and set aside their prejudices, should read it.

Overview

Synopsis of the Following Six Meditations (pp. 54–6)

Descartes explains that the *First* Meditation deals with why
we can doubt everything and the value of doing so, which is
to remove prejudices, withdraw the mind from the influence
of the senses, and make it impossible to doubt things later
discovered to be true. In the *Second*, the mind supposes the
non-existence of everything it can doubt, so as to distinguish
between what belongs to the intellect and the body. The *Third*
contains his principal argument for God's existence. The
Fourth proves that everything that is clearly and distinctly
perceived is true. The *Fifth* explains corporeal nature, and has
a further proof of God's existence. The *Sixth* distinguishes
the understanding from the imagination; proves that mind
and body are distinct; sets out the errors arising from the
senses; and discusses the arguments from which we infer the
existence of material things.

*Meditations on First Philosophy in which the Existence of
God and the Distinction Between the Soul and the Body Are
Demonstrated*

Meditation One: Concerning those Things that Can Be Called Into Doubt (pp. 59–63)

The need to doubt everything (Cartesian doubt)

Years before, Descartes had realized he held many false
opinions, which he regarded as true, and that, to be certain
of anything, he needed to start again. He decides to withhold
assent from uncertain and doubtful opinions, as well as clearly
false ones. Those he regards as most true come through the
senses, but they can deceive. Some things, such as his belief

47

that he is now looking at his hands, seem beyond doubt. But, when he is asleep, he dreams about all sorts of things, and there are no definitive signs by which to distinguish being awake from being asleep.

But, even if he is dreaming, the things he sees resemble true things, and things in thought are created from things in the real world. So, such simple and universal things as corporeal nature and extension do seem to be true. This must mean that, although a discipline like physics, which deals with composite things, is doubtful, one involving the simplest and most general things, such as arithmetic, has some certainty. Asleep or awake, two plus three equals five.

What if an all-powerful God is deceiving him?

But what if an all-powerful God has so ordered it that no earth or anything else exists, but things still appear to exist as they do now? Of course, God is said to be supremely good, and may not have willed his being deceived all the time. But, in that case, why is he deceived sometimes? Some would rather deny the existence of an all-powerful God than believe everything else is uncertain. However, the less powerful God is, the more likely it is that human beings are imperfect and always deceived. So, to be certain of anything, he needs to withhold assent from all his former beliefs, even though they still seem highly probable. He must treat them as wholly false, so that nothing prevents his achieving the correct perception of things.

He will believe that an evil genius is deceiving him

Instead of a supremely good God, he will believe that an evil genius is deceiving him. He will treat all apparently external things, including heaven and earth, as illusions, and think of himself as without body or senses, but deceived into believing he has them. This will ensure his withholding assent from anything false, and stop the evil genius tricking him.

Meditation Two: Concerning the Nature of the Human Mind: That It Is Better Known than the Body (pp. 63–9)

Even if he is being deceived, he exists, if he is being deceived

One thing that does not seem doubtful is that there is a God, who gives him these thoughts. But, he may be their author himself, which means he is something. He may deny the existence of his body, senses and the external world but, if he can persuade himself of something, he does exist. Even if an all-powerful God is deceiving him, he exists, if he is being deceived. He is not nothing, while he thinks he is something. So, the statement that he is, is necessarily true every time he thinks it.

He is nothing but a thinking thing

But what is he? His first thought used to be that he had a body. However, if an all-powerful God is deceiving him, he cannot be certain of anything to do with the body. Thinking, on the other hand, cannot be separated from him. As long as he thinks, he exists; if he stopped thinking, he would cease to exist. He is nothing but a thinking thing. He is the one doubting almost everything, but who observes many things that seem to come from the senses. Even if God is deceiving him, he is the one doubting, understanding and imagining, and who is aware of physical things, as if through the senses. He still cannot help thinking that physical things are known more distinctly than this 'I'. But, it would be odd to understand the things he doubts better than he understands himself.

The piece of wax

Descartes considers bodies. A piece of hard, cold wax seems to have all the properties needed for it to be known. But, held close to the fire, it becomes hot and liquid. He wonders if it is the same piece of wax, as none of its previous properties remain. He asks what is left – only something that is extended, flexible and mutable. He realizes that wax can undergo many changes, but this realization comes through his mind. This is something he needs to grasp – what he understands about the wax is not to do with seeing, touching or imagining, but with the mind alone.

However, his mind can be mistaken, due to the way things are discussed. We say we see the wax itself, not that we judge it to be present from its colour or shape. This suggests knowledge through seeing, rather than mental inspection. It was with his mind that he distinguished the wax from its external forms, and saw it as it is. He concludes that, however he judges that the wax exists, it cannot be the case that, while he does so he, who is thinking, is not something. He knows that even physical things are not perceived by the senses, but by the intellect. Therefore, there is nothing he can perceive with less difficulty than his own mind.

Meditation Three: Concerning God, that He Exists (pp. 69–81)

What he sees clearly and distinctly is true

He will treat all images of physical things as false, to help him to know himself better. He is a thing that thinks, and even if the things he senses do not exist outside him, the modes of thinking relating to them exist within him. There is nothing in this first piece of knowledge but a clear and distinct perception of what he affirms, but it seems he can take it as a general rule that what he sees clearly and distinctly is true. However, he used to acknowledge as certain things he later found to be doubtful, such as those perceived through the senses. He knows that he has ideas of these things, but used to think that he clearly perceived that the ideas came from external objects.

He must establish whether God exists, whether or not he is a deceiver, and classify his thoughts, to distinguish the true from the false

Something like two and three making five seems clear enough to be affirmed as true. He only doubted such things, because he thought an all-powerful God might be deceiving him. But, even such a God could not make two plus three not add up to five, because it would be contradictory. He has no evidence that God is a deceiver (or even exists), so his doubts about God have no firm basis. To progress with his enquiries, he must establish whether God exists, and whether or not he is a deceiver.

He must classify his thoughts, to distinguish the true from the false. Taken in isolation, his ideas cannot be false. Whatever he imagines or chooses, he is definitely imagining or choosing it. His main error, when judging, is thinking his ideas conform to things outside himself. But, there can be no error, if he just regards them as different modes of thought, some of which seem innate, while others seem to come from external sources. However, his natural impulse to believe that some ideas come from external sources does not mean they do. Their appearing independently of his will does not necessarily make their source external. They may come from within, like those in dreams. And, even if they have external sources, it does not follow that they resemble them. The sun looks small, but astronomy shows that it is larger than the earth; and both ideas cannot be right. This suggests that his belief that external things send him ideas through his senses has a shaky basis.

The idea of an infinite and omnipotent God, who made everything, is more objectively real than those relating to finite substances

Another approach is that ideas involving substances have more objective reality than those representing modes or accidents, while the idea of an infinite and omnipotent God, who made everything, is more objectively real than those relating to finite substances. An effect's reality comes from its cause. A thing cannot come into being from nothing, nor can something more perfect from something less perfect. An idea containing something not in the cause would be getting something from nothing.

Further, although one idea can come from another, there cannot be an infinite regress: there must be a first idea. His ideas are like images – they may not equal, but cannot exceed, the perfection of the things from which they derive. If an idea's objective reality is too great to have originated in him, it necessarily follows that he is not alone in the world. If not, he cannot be certain that anything, other than himself, exists.

As well as that of himself, his ideas include those of God, physical things, animals and other humans. He might have derived his ideas of humans and animals from those he has of God, himself and physical things.

He is a finite substance, which does not account for his idea of an infinite substance

But his idea of God, the infinite and omnipotent creator, cannot have started in him. Although he has the idea of substance, because he is a substance, he is finite, which does not account for his idea of infinite substance. And, as the idea must have come from an infinite substance, he must conclude that God necessarily exists. Indeed, his perception of God is prior to that of himself; he is aware of his own defects through having the idea of a more perfect being. As his most clear and distinct idea, it is the least likely to be false. He could pretend such a being does not exist, but not that the idea of it indicates nothing real. This idea contains everything he recognizes as involving some perfection. His not understanding the infinite is beside the point, because this is not attainable by one who is finite. His idea of God is the most true, clear and distinct he has.

Could he himself have the perfections he ascribes to God potentially?

However, he could have the perfections he ascribes to God potentially. His increasing knowledge could reach infinity, giving him the idea of perfections. But, there is nothing potential in God. The fact that his own knowledge increases proves his own imperfection while, as God is infinite, his perfection cannot be added to. His mind is overwhelmed by sensible things, so he overlooks the fact that the idea of a being more perfect than him must come from one who actually is. If he got his being from himself, he would be God. In which case, he would have given himself all the perfections contained in the idea of God, none of which would have been harder to acquire than for him, a thinking substance, to emerge out of nothing.

A cause cannot be inferior to its effect

He could suppose he had always existed. But, as the same power is needed to preserve as to create something, it would not follow, from his existing a short time ago, that he must exist now, unless there is a preserving cause. As a thinking thing, if he had the power to ensure his continued existence, he would be aware of it, so he must depend upon another being. As a cause cannot be inferior to its effect, his parents, or a less perfect cause than God, could not have produced him. As a thinking thing, with the idea of God, his cause must be a thinking thing with an idea of all the perfections he ascribes to God. If this cause's existence came from itself, it is God because, with the power of existing in and of itself, it possesses all the perfections he ascribes to God. If its existence came from another cause, he will persist until he reaches the ultimate cause – God. There can be no infinite regress, as he is concerned with the cause that produced and preserves him. He cannot be the product of several causes, because one of the chief perfections he understands God to possess is unity and simplicity.

His existing and having an idea of a most perfect being show that God exists

The facts of his existing, and having an idea of a most perfect being, show that God exists. His idea of God did not come from the senses, nor did he make it, so it must be innate. As God made him, it is all the more credible that God should have made him in his image and likeness, and that he sees this likeness with the same faculty by which he perceives himself. So, when he thinks about himself, he recognizes his own incompleteness and dependence on a being, who possesses all the things to which he aspires. He could not exist, and have the idea of God, unless God existed; and, as deception comes from a defect, of which God has none, clearly he does not deceive.

Meditation Four: Concerning the True and the False (pp. 81–7)

He seems to occupy a middle ground between being and non-being

In withdrawing his mind from the senses, Descartes has noticed he perceives more about the mind than physical things. When focusing on himself as incomplete and dependent, he has a clear and distinct idea of God. From having this idea, he concludes that God, on whom he depends, also exists. He now sees a way to progress to knowledge of other things. God does not deceive him, and he has a God-given faculty of judgement, which will not mislead him, if used properly. He feels he should be incapable of error, and is, when thinking about God. However, he makes many errors when thinking about himself. He seems to occupy a middle ground between God and non-being. As God's creation, he can only be led into error by participating in non-being, as he does not have an infinite faculty of judgement. He wonders why God did not make him error-free. However, God, who is infinite, does things for reasons he does not understand. It is no reason for doubting God's existence. When considering God's works, people should not focus on an apparent imperfection in part of the universe, but on how it may fit into the general scheme of things.

The intellect and the will

His errors arise from the relationship between intellect and will. The former just enables him to perceive ideas, about which he can make a judgement and, at that level, is free of error (although there may be many things he does not know about, he cannot prove that God should have given him more knowledge than he has). His will, unlike his other faculties (which contrast with those of God, whose faculties are infinite) has no limitations. Indeed, his will is the basis for his understanding that he has been made in God's image, because God's faculty of willing does not seem greater than his. Willing is being able to do or not to do something suggested by the intellect, without the decision being determined by any external force. This does not mean that a person is not free, when inclined to make one decision, rather than another, as divine grace or natural knowledge may enable him to recognize what is right; and this actually makes a person more free.

The will extends beyond the intellect, which can lead to error

It is not his powers of willing and understanding, by themselves, that lead to error, but the fact that his will extends beyond his intellect, to matters he does not understand. This can result in his making mistakes, and not doing what is right. His present examination of whether anything exists in the world illustrates the point. He concluded that he existed from the very fact that he was making this examination. However, he felt compelled to judge that his conclusion was true, not because of an external force, but because intellectual enlightenment gave way to a great inclination of the will. He knows that, as a thinking thing, he exists, but not whether his thinking and physical natures are different or the same; neither alternative seems intellectually convincing. With such difficult questions, he will be using his freedom properly, if he reaches a judgement only when he sees the truth with clarity and distinctness.

God cannot be blamed for his mistaken judgements

He cannot complain that God has not given him greater powers of understanding, as it is the essence of a finite intellect to not understand many things; instead, he must thank God for what he does understand. Nor can he complain that the scope of his will is wider than that of his intellect; it is indivisible, so nothing could be removed from it.

He cannot blame God for his own mistaken judgements. Insofar as they depend on God, they are true and good, while it is better to be able to make such judgements than not. It is no imperfection in God that God has made him free to give or withhold assent in matters about which God has not given him a clear and distinct perception; he must refrain from judging things he does not understand properly. God could have ensured that he was never mistaken, without limiting his freedom, or giving him more than finite knowledge – by giving him a clear and distinct perception in every matter he considers, or made him so that he always applied the rule of not judging anything he does not understand clearly and distinctly.

The universe may be more perfect through having some error-prone parts

But, although that might have made him more perfect, the universe may be more perfect with some error-prone parts than none. He must not complain that God has not given him a perfect part in it. He can avoid error by always applying the rule of not judging a matter unless it is clear. Every clear and distinct perception does not come from nothing and, necessarily, God must be its author. He will attain truth only by attending carefully to the things he perfectly understands, and distinguishing them from those he does not.

Meditation Five: Concerning the Essence of Material Things, and Again Concerning God, that He Exists (pp. 87–92)

Is there any certainty about material things?

Descartes wonders if there is any certainty about material things. Before trying to decide, he needs to identify any distinct ideas about them. He can imagine things with length, breadth and depth and, as he focuses on them, seems to be recalling what he already knew. Even if they do not exist outside him, they cannot be regarded as nothing. When he imagines a triangle, even if no such thing exists outside his thought, its essence is independent of his mind. It has such properties as three angles that are equal to two right angles, irrespective of what he thinks. It is irrelevant to say that the idea came to him through his senses, because he can demonstrate the properties of other figures that certainly did not. These properties are obviously true, because he knows them clearly; and, indeed, he had previously regarded the truths of pure and abstract mathematics as the most certain of all.

An ontological proof of God's existence

But, if he can derive the idea of something from thought, and it follows that what he clearly and distinctly perceives as belonging to it does, this can be used to prove God's existence. The idea of God is no less within him than that of any number, and he perceives that his always existing belongs to God's nature just as clearly and distinctly. Therefore, he should be as certain of God's existence as of mathematical truths. However, as he can distinguish existence from essence with all other things, he can persuade himself that this is also so with God, and that he can be thought of as not existing. But, anyone thinking carefully about the matter can see that it is no more possible to separate existence from God's essence than to separate its having three angles equal to two right angles from the essence of a triangle. It is contradictory to think that God, who is supremely perfect, lacks the perfection of existence.

Existence is inseparable from God, so he really exists

However, although he cannot think of a mountain without a valley, this does not mean that a mountain or valley exists, only that, whether they exist or not, they cannot be separated from each other. But, from the fact that he cannot think of God, except as existing, it follows that existence is inseparable from God, and so he really exists. This is not a case of thought imposing necessity on anything; it is the necessity of God's existence that compels him to think it. He might never think about God but, if he does, he must ascribe every perfection to him. As existence is a perfection, he rightly concludes that God exists. It is to God's essence alone that existence belongs, and there could not be more than one such God. He sees clearly the necessity of God's having existed from, and enduring for, eternity; and that God has many other features that he cannot remove or change.

Nothing can be more obvious than God's existence, and God is no deceiver

He returns to the point that he is only fully convinced by things he perceives clearly and distinctly. Some of these are fairly obvious, while others require careful enquiry but, once discovered, are regarded as certain. As for God, it is only his prejudices and the insistent images of sensible things that make it hard to see that he exists. Nothing can be more obvious than God's existence, to whose essence alone existence belongs.

One problem is that, although he believes something to be true, while he is clearly and distinctly perceiving it, he cannot always maintain concentration on it. As a result, if he were ignorant of God, he might, on hearing counter-arguments, start to doubt what he had clearly perceived. But, once he saw that God is no deceiver, he concluded that what he sees clearly and distinctly is necessarily true, so no counter-argument can make him doubt it. He now knows how to determine truth – if anything is evident to his intellect, it is entirely true. Thus, every science's truth and certainty depends on knowledge of God, and he can now achieve certain knowledge of many things, including God, other intellectual matters and corporeal nature.

Meditation Six: Concerning the Existence of Material Things, and the Real Distinction Between Mind and Body (pp. 92–103)

The existence of material things

Descartes turns to the existence of material things. He knows they exist as objects of pure mathematics, because he clearly and distinctly perceives this; he can also imagine them. He considers the difference between imagination and pure intellection. If he imagines a triangle, he understands it to be a three-sided figure and can also picture it. But, if he thinks about a thousand-sided figure, he does not picture it. Thus, imagining requires a peculiar sort of mental effort, which understanding does not.

Unlike understanding, the ability to imagine is not necessary to the essence of his mind. When the mind understands something, it turns towards itself, and examines one of the ideas in it. But, when it imagines something, it turns to the body, and intuits in it something that conforms to an idea that it understands, or that the senses perceive. This suggests that bodies exist, but he still does not see how it necessarily follows, from his imagination's idea of bodily nature, that some body does exist. However, he imagines many things, such as colours and sounds, which seem to have come to his imagination via the senses. He wonders if he can base an argument for the existence of physical things on sense perception. He will need to examine the matter carefully, to determine what he used to think true, because he perceived them through the senses; why he came to doubt them; and what he believes now.

He will avoid hasty belief in the information that seems to come from the senses, without doubting all of it

He used to believe he had, or was, a body among many others; judged what was bad or good for him through sensations of pain and pleasure; became hungry and thirsty; and experienced bodily tendencies to, for example, mirth and sadness. As well as their extension, he sensed bodies' tactile qualities and also light, colour and sound, enabling him to distinguish one body from another. Thus, not surprisingly, he sensed things clearly different from thought – the bodies from which these ideas came. It seemed impossible that the ideas originated in him, because they were more vivid than any formed in thought, or found in memory. Further, he could not stop them coming to him, and they only did so when an object was present to one of his sense organs. Therefore, he concluded they came from external objects. Also, there seemed good reason to believe that one particular body belonged to him. He could not separate himself from it, and was aware of pain and pleasure in parts of it, but not in external bodies. He had wondered why a certain sensation, such as hunger, should alert him to the need to eat. The answer seemed to be that nature had taught him so.

However, experience had undermined his faith in the senses, as they were often wrong. Things that appeared round from a distance seemed square at close quarters. What he thought he sensed while awake, he also seemed to sense while asleep. As he did not believe that the latter came from external objects, he began to doubt that the former did. Being ignorant of God, there was nothing to stop him thinking that he might be wrong about things that appeared to be true. He started to doubt what nature had taught him, and to think that some unknown faculty inside him produced perceptions of what appeared to be external objects. However, now that he knows himself and God better, he will avoid hasty belief in the information that seems to come from the senses, without doubting all of it.

As God does not deceive, his ideas of sensible things must come from external objects

The first thing he knows is that God can make all the things he clearly and distinctly understands in the way he understands them. So, as he can understand one thing separately from another, he can be certain that they actually are separate. As he knows that he exists, and that the only thing that belongs to his essence is that he is a thinking thing, he knows this is his essence. No doubt, he will soon be able to say that he has a body closely joined to him, but he will also be certain that he is distinct from it, and can exist without it. Further, he has faculties of imagining and sensing, which could not exist without him, a substance that has understanding. He has other faculties, such as the ability to move from place to place, but these require a body. He also has a passive faculty of sensing, which receives ideas of sensible things.

However, he would be unable to use it without an active faculty, which produces these ideas. This cannot be in him, because he does not control production of the ideas, so it must be in a different substance: external objects, God, or another creature. As God does not deceive, he does not send him these ideas himself, or via another creature. Indeed, God has strongly inclined him to believe they come from physical objects, so these exist. He may make mistakes about them, but they are what he clearly and distinctly understands them to be; and the fact that God is not a deceiver gives him hope of discovering the truth about matters that remain uncertain.

There is no reason to doubt the truth of what nature teaches us

Descartes sees no reason to doubt the truth of what nature teaches, as it is the ordered network of created things God has established. Nature uses such sensations as pain and hunger to teach that body and thinking self are one single thing. If they were not, he would perceive his own bodily injury intellectually, not through the sensation of pain, and would understand that he needed food intellectually, not as a result of feeling hungry. He is aware of other bodies around him, and perceives that he (comprising body and mind) is adversely or beneficially affected by them. However, although nature teaches us to avoid things that cause pain, for example, it does not teach us to draw any conclusions from sense perceptions; this requires intellectual enquiry into external objects. A star seems the same size as a flame, and there is no indication in the perception that it is larger. In general, sense perceptions are reliable guides to external bodies, but the information they give can be confused. Indeed, errors occur, even when nature drives us towards things, as when a sick person wants food or drink, which would harm him. It is hard to accept that God gave us our error-prone nature, or to understand why he allows us to be deceived.

The difference between mind and body

A significant point is the great difference between the mind and the body. The body is divisible into parts, whereas the mind is indivisible. Further, the only part of the body that affects the mind is the brain: in particular, the small part where common sense is located. When this part of the brain is inclined in a particular way, it presents the same thing to the mind, irrespective of what else is going on in the body. Further, if a person feels a pain in one part of his body, the sensation is conveyed along the nerves to the brain, and affects the mind with a sensation of pain. But, as the nerves pass through other parts of the body, the same sensation will occur in the brain, and the mind will experience the same pain, which can be misleading. However, as any movement in the part of the brain affecting the mind gives rise to only one sensation, it is best that it is pain, which helps to preserve human beings; and this testifies to God's goodness. Again, it is generally beneficial to human health to have a sensation of thirst when a drink is needed, even if it is not so in the case of someone with dropsy.

Despite God's goodness, human beings are bound to make mistakes

Descartes concludes that, despite God's goodness, human beings, consisting of mind and body, are bound to make mistakes. In general, the senses more often indicate what is true than not but, to avoid error, human beings must make full use of all their faculties. He can dismiss his recent extreme doubts. As for distinguishing between being asleep and being awake, memory does not connect the things in dreams with other things in life, nor do they happen in predictable ways. As God is no deceiver, he cannot be mistaken, if he enquires carefully into things, although lack of time means that human beings are bound to make mistakes on occasions.

Glossary

Ability to choose freely. Descartes maintains (Meditation Four) that the human will is completely free – the human faculty of willing is equal to God's.

Accident(s). A property of something that is not part of its essence, and which could be added to, or taken away from, it without it ceasing to be the same thing.

Annihilation of the mind. Destruction, elimination of the mind. In the *Meditations* Descartes argues that, as mind and body are separate, and the mind, unlike the body, is indivisible, bodily death does not involve destruction of the mind.

Anselm, Saint (1033–1109). Italian-born philosopher and theologian, his writings include the *Monologion* and *Proslogion*. Anselm was Abbot of the Norman Abbey of Bec, and succeeded Lanfranc as Archbishop of Canterbury in 1093.

Aquinas, Saint Thomas (c. 1225–74). Italian-born philosopher and theologian and Dominican friar, whose setting forth of Roman Catholic teaching was declared definitive by Pope Leo XIII. His books include the *Summa Theologica* (*Summa Theologiae*), the *Summa Contra Gentiles* and the *De Veritate*.

Archetype. Original model, which determines the form of other things.

Ascribing human emotions to God. Descartes (Preface to the

Reader) accuses atheists of anthropomorphism (treating God as human-like).

Astronomical reasoning/astronomy. Scientific study of stars/ heavenly bodies. This shows that conclusions about the heavenly bodies, based purely on sense experience, cannot be trusted (Meditation Three).

Atheist. One who is convinced that there is no God, as opposed to an agnostic, who merely doubts God's existence.

Attribute(s). Properties, characteristics. Those of the Christian God include omnipotence and omniscience.

Author of my existence. Cause of my existence – God.

Bedevilling hoaxes. Devilish and confusing deceptions.

Bodies' tactile qualities. Bodies' ability to be experienced, and known about, through the sense of touch.

Cartesian doubt. Descartes' extreme and comprehensive doubt of everything he previously believed, in order to discover what is certain. See also Pyrrho of Elis below.

Cause. That which brings about a certain effect.

Cause of God and religion. Descartes maintains that his proofs of God's existence and the immortality of the soul will refute atheist arguments, and promote and strengthen religious belief.

Certain and evident knowledge of the truth. In the *Meditations*, Descartes is concerned with establishing what can certainly be known.

Chiliagon. Thousand-sided figure in geometry.

Clear and distinct perception. Descartes concludes (Meditation Three) that he can take it as a general rule that what he sees clearly and distinctly is true.

Common sense. In the *Meditations*, this refers to a sense with the specific task of co-ordinating information provided by the other senses.

Composite. Something made up of parts.

Contradiction. When a proposition and its negation are brought together, as would be the case (Meditation Three) if it were stated that two plus three both did, and did not, add up to five.

Corporeal nature. Bodily, physical nature.

Created/creation. According to Christian teaching, God created the universe and all it contains from nothing.

Creature(s). Something created, including, if God made the world, human beings.

Dean and Doctors of the Faculty of Sacred Theology of Paris. In his Letter of Dedication, Descartes seeks the Sorbonne's support for the *Meditations*, in order to ensure their favourable reception.

Defect(s). Fault, shortcoming. Descartes is made aware of his own defects, as a human being, through having the idea of a more perfect being – God (Meditation Three).

Demonstrate. Prove something conclusively.

Discourse on Method. Descartes' *Discourse on the Method for Conducting One's Reason Well and for Seeking Truth in the Sciences*, published in 1637.

Divisible/indivisible. Capable of being divided/incapable of being divided. Descartes held that the body is divisible (and so mortal), whereas the soul/mind is indivisible (and so immortal).

Dream(s). Part of Descartes' doubt about the existence of the external world relates (Meditation One) to the apparent absence of any definitive signs by which to distinguish the things he dreams from the things he is actually experiencing. However, he concludes (Meditation Six) that memory does not connect things in dreams with other things in life, in a coherent way, nor do events in dreams occur in a predictable manner.

Dropsy. Disease in which watery fluid collects in parts of the body.

Effect. That which results from, is produced by, a cause. Descartes argues (Meditation Three) that something cannot come into being from nothing, nor can a thing be the cause of something that is more perfect than itself.

Emerge out of nothing. Descartes believes (Meditation Three) that he, a thinking thing, cannot have emerged out of nothing. The cause that produced and preserves him must be a thinking thing with the power of existing in and of itself – God.

Empiricist. Philosopher who believes that (sense) experience is the (principal) source of knowledge. See rationalist, senses and sensible things below.

Essence. The essential nature of something, that which makes something what it is, and without which it would not be what it is.

Eternal. Without beginning or end, lasting for ever. In a religious context, the idea that God transcends time. There is no past, present or future in God, who endures beyond every kind of given duration.

Evil genius. Descartes' device (Meditation One) to ensure that he really is discarding all his previous basic beliefs, in order to find something that is certainly true. He takes it that a wicked and all-powerful being is using all its skill to deceive him.

Extension (physical). That physical things are extended and occupy space.

Extensive doubt. See Cartesian doubt above.

External force. Outside force, force outside ourselves.

External things. Things that exist in the world around us, about which our senses give us information. Cartesian doubt (see above) involves doubting the existence of an external world and anything that exists independently of the mind.

Faculty. Power, power of the mind.

Faculty of Judgement. Power, ability to judge.

Faith. In a religious context, this can be simply religious belief/belief in God, or trusting belief in God (his existence and/or goodness), which is not supported by clear evidence or convincing philosophical arguments.

Finite. Limited.

Finite substance(s). Beings with limited powers, unlike God, whose powers are infinite.

First philosophy. Fundamental philosophical issues – the *Meditations* concern the existence of God and the immortality of the soul.

Formal reality. If a cause produces an effect of the same nature as itself, that nature must be formally present in the cause (Meditation Three).

Geometry. Science/study of the properties and relations of lines, angles, surfaces and solids. Descartes took a leading part in the development of the subject.

God. In the *Meditations*, the Christian God.

God necessarily exists. God cannot not-exist. Descartes believes that his arguments in Meditations Three and Five prove this.

God's existence. Descartes maintains that God's existence can be proved by philosophical argument, and offers two proofs: that our idea of a supremely perfect being, God, must come from God (Meditation Three); and his version of the ontological argument (Meditation Five).

Grace. The help God freely gives to human beings through Jesus Christ; the means of understanding and accepting in faith what God has revealed of himself to human beings.

Hobbes, Thomas (1588–1679). British philosopher and author of the *Elements of Law, Human Nature* and *Leviathan*.

Holy Scriptures. The Bible. Descartes accepts (Letter of Dedication) that people should believe that God exists on the basis of what he has revealed to them in the Bible, but unbelievers want philosophical proof(s).

Human philosophy. Philosophy, as opposed to theology.

Hypothesis. A theory put forward as a basis for reasoning, or starting-point for discussion.

Idea of a thing more perfect than me. See God's existence above.

Image(s). Likeness or copy.

Image and likeness (of God). According to Genesis 1:26, human beings are made in the image or likeness of God.

Imagination. The human ability to form images or pictures in the mind. Descartes concludes (Meditation Six) that this ability, unlike that of understanding, is not necessary to the essence of his mind.

Immortality (of the soul). The idea that the soul (which Descartes argues is indivisible) does not die, but lives on for ever.

Immutable. Unchangeable.

Incomprehensible. That which cannot be understood. God is ultimately incomprehensible to finite human minds.

Infinite. Unlimited, without limit.

Infinite regress (of causes and effects). Sequence of cause and effects, which has no beginning or end.

Infinite substance. God. Descartes argues (Meditation Three) that his (a finite substance) idea of infinite substance (God) must have come from an infinite substance (God).

Infinity. Infinite quantity.

Innate. That which is inborn. Descartes distinguishes (Meditation Three) between ideas that seem innate and ones that seem to come from experience of objects in the external world.

Intellect. See mind below.

Intellection. Thinking.

Intellectual nature. See mind below.

Intermediate. Located between.

Intuit. Know by intuition – an immediate mental apprehension/awareness.

Kant, Immanuel (1724–1804). Influential German philosopher, whose writings cover metaphysics, moral philosophy and philosophy of religion, and include the *Critique of Pure Reason*, the *Critique of Practical Reason*, *Religion Within the Boundaries of Mere Reason* and the *Groundwork of the Metaphysics of Morals*.

Kristina Wasa (1626–89). Daughter of King Gustav II and Queen of Sweden from 1632 until her abdication in 1654, she had extensive intellectual interests, including philosophy and ethics.

Lateran Council. Councils of the Roman Catholic Church, which took place at the Lateran Palace in Rome. Descartes refers to the Fifth Lateran Council (1512–17), which was summoned by Pope Julius II, and continued under Leo X.

Leo X (1475–1521). Giovanni di Lorenzo de Medici was Pope from 1513 to 1521. Pope when Martin Luther protested about the sale of indulgences in Germany, he excommunicated him in 1520.

Malicious deceiver. See evil genius above.

Material things. Things in the material world, physical things, things made of matter.

Mathematics. Science/study of space and numbers. Descartes took a leading part in the development of the subject.

Matter. That of which the universe consists apart from mind/spirit.

Mediation. Acting as a go-between. Having concluded that he is not being deceived by an evil genius, Descartes (Meditation Six) rejects the possibilities that his ideas of external objects are given to him directly by God, or come from God, through the mediation of another creature – they must come from physical objects.

Memory. The mind's ability to recall things from the past. Descartes notes (Meditation Six) that the ideas in his memory are less vivid and explicit than those experienced when an object is present to one of his sense organs.

Metaphysical. See metaphysical studies/metaphysics below.

Metaphysical studies/metaphysics. Study of what is after (beyond) physics, and which cannot be investigated by ordinary empirical methods; the investigation of what really exists, of ultimate reality.

Middle ground between the supreme being and non-being. This is the position that Descartes considers he occupies as a thinking thing (Meditation Four). It arises from the medieval/scholastic idea that things do not just either exist or not exist, but that there are levels or grades of being, and that God is the supreme being and the cause of all other beings.

Mind. What Descartes (Meditation Two) concludes that he really is – a thinking thing, a mind or reason.

Mode(s) of thinking/thought. (Different) ways of thinking.

Mutable. Capable of change, likely to change.

Natural impulse. Inborn, instinctive tendency.

Nature. Descartes concludes that, as nature is the ordered network of created things that God has established, it is possible to rely upon what it teaches us through such sensations as pain and hunger (Meditation Six).

Nature of God. God is infinite, and his faculties/powers are unlimited.

Nature of the soul. See mind above and soul below.

Necessarily true. That which must be true, and which could not be otherwise.

Non-believer/unbeliever(s). One who does not believe in God.

Objective reality. Actual reality.

Omnipotent. God's power is unlimited, so he is all-powerful or omnipotent.

Omniscient. God's knowledge is infinite, so he is all-knowing or omniscient.

Only natural reason can convince non-believers of religious truths. Those who do not believe in God's existence will not start to do so on the basis of faith in God's revelation. They need to be convinced by philosophical arguments.

Ontological argument. One of the traditional arguments for the existence of God, which argues from the concept of God to his existence. It was first put forward by Anselm (*Proslogion*), but was rejected by Thomas Aquinas (*Summa Theologica*). Descartes (in a version that differs from Anselm's) revives it in the *Meditations*, and it is Descartes' version that Kant refutes in the *Critique of Pure Reason*.

Patently false. Manifestly untrue.

Perception/perceive. Be, become aware of (something). A rationalist, Descartes holds (Meditation Two) that it is through his mind, not his senses, that he becomes aware of the properties of a piece of wax.

Perfect/perfection(s). Complete, without fault, quality that is without fault. Descartes argues (Meditation Five) that, as God is supremely perfect, he must possess the perfection of existence – a view repudiated by Kant in his *Critique of Pure Reason*.

Philosopher. One who studies and practises/teaches philosophy.

Philosophy. Literally, love of wisdom. The study of ultimate reality, what really exists, the most general principles of things.

Potentially. That which could become the case.

Power of existing in and of itself. God's existence comes from himself; he was not caused by anything else, nor does his existence depend on anything else (aseity).

Powerful (of God). See omnipotent.

Prejudice(s). Opinion formed about something on the basis of inadequate knowledge or experience of it.

Prerequisite. Something required as a condition of something else.

Preserving cause. God is the preserver/sustainer, as well as the creator.

Principal argument for God's existence. The argument Descartes puts forward in Meditation Two. See also God's existence above.

Pure substance. The mind is pure substance, as there are no accidents in it. It is pure substance, and indivisible, and so, unlike the body, cannot perish.

Pyrrho of Elis (c. 365–275 BC). Greek philosopher, who established a profoundly sceptical approach to philosophical enquiry. His ideas became influential in France from the mid-sixteenth century, following publication of the works of Sextus Empiricus.

Rational animal. What Descartes (Meditation Two) thought he really was before he started to doubt all his beliefs. See mind above.

Rationalist. A philosopher, like Descartes, who believes that reason, rather than (sense) experience is the (principal) source of knowledge.

Reason. The mind, the ability to think.

Reveals/revelation. What God chooses to disclose of himself to human beings, through, for example, prophets and holy scriptures.

Scholastic/scholasticism. The Christian-centred philosophy, taught in medieval universities, of which Aquinas was one of the leading exponents.

Sensation(s). Consciousness of something, feeling.

Sensations of pain and pleasure. Feelings of pain and pleasure.

Senses. Sight, hearing, touch, taste and smell, which give us access to, and knowledge of, things in the world around us.

Sensible things. The things we have access to, and acquire knowledge of, through our senses.

Several partial causes. Descartes rejects the idea (Meditation Three) that he has been produced by a combination of finite causes, as opposed to God, one of whose chief perfections is unity and simplicity.

Sextus Empiricus (first–second century AD). Greek medical practitioner and philosopher, whose writings include *Outlines of Pyrrhonism*. See Pyrrho of Elis above.

Simple/simplicity. Not consisting of parts, not composite – God is simple.

Sin. Offence against, disobedience of, God.

Sorbonne. The Collège de Sorbonne was founded by Robert de Sorbon in the twelfth century as a college for theology students. One of the colleges of the University of Paris, it served as its Faculty of Theology.

Soul. In Christianity, the spiritual element within human beings, which is the seat of personality and individual identity, which lives on after death, and which will be reunited with its body at the general resurrection. In his Second Meditation, Descartes attempts to prove (and believes he has succeeded in doing so) that soul and body are completely separate.

Spirit of contrariness. Perverse attitude, inclination (always) to disagree – an attitude Descartes attributes (Letter of Dedication) to atheists.

Substance. The essence of something, which makes it what it is.

Supreme deity. God.

Supremely good. According to Christian teaching, God is infinitely good/loving.

Supremely perfect being. God. Descartes argues (Meditation Three) that the idea of a supremely perfect being can only come from a supremely perfect cause.

Supremely perfect cause. God. See supremely perfect being above.

Tenuous. Thin, slender.

Theologian. One who studies and practises/teaches theology.

Theology. Generally, setting out the beliefs and teachings of a religion in a systematic way; academic discipline concerned with the study of religion/religious beliefs and teachings.

Thinking thing. See mind above.

Treatise(s). Book or paper that deals with a specific subject in a systematic way.

Ultimate cause. God.

Unity. Oneness. God is perfect oneness, one reality.

Universal(s). A general characteristic or quality of things, such as redness or roundness, of which specific things are instances.

Universal scheme of things. The way God has ordered things in the world he has created. Descartes (Meditation Three) warns against concentrating on (and criticizing) what appear to be particular flaws in the universe, when they may have their part to play in the wider scheme of things.

Volition(s). Act of willing.

Will. The capability of wishing for something and using one's mental powers to try to accomplish it.

Works of God. What God has created – the universe and all it contains.

The Briefly Series